1,2&3 COLOR Graphics

P·I·E BOOKS

1, 2 & 3 COLOR GRAPHICS

1, 2 & 3 COLOR Graphics

EDITORIAL NOTES:
CD: Creative Director AD: Art Director D: Designer
P: Photographer I: Illustrator CW: Copywriter
DF: Design Firm CL: Client

本文クレジット中、会社名については株式（有限）会社、Company Limited、Incorporated 等の表記を省略しました。
The words "Company Limited" and "Incorporated" have been omitted from the credits in this book.
国名は出品者の居住国を表記しました。
The country indicated for each entry is the country in which the submittor resides.

作品提供者の情報をもとに各作品の刷色を色サンプルとして作品データ欄に記載しました。また作品提供者の情報が不足しているものに関しては当社の判断により記載しました。特別な色に関しては色サンプルの中に下記のように略字で表示しました。
In this book, color samples are given in the artwork data section for printing colors used. This information is based upon that provided by the submittors. In cases where little or no such information was provided, we prepared the artwork data section based upon our own judgement. To indicate special effects or specialty inks, we have included codes within the color samples, as shown below.

Gold 金色→G Silver 銀色→S Copper 銅色→C Matte Black マット黒→M B
Varnish / Clear Varnish / Matte Varnish ニス→V Fluorescent ink 蛍光色→F
Thermography バーコ印刷→T Hot Stamps 箔押し→H Metallic ink パールインク→M

本書は4色プロセスで印刷をしていますので、色サンプルが実際の刷色と多少異なる場合があります。また作品に関する情報が少なかったものに関しては当社が最大限の努力をして判断しましたことをご了承ください。
As this book is printed using standard 4-color process inks, there may be some instances in which the color samples given are slightly different from the actual printed colors. As for those artworks which came with little or no relevant color information to accompany them. However, we will not be held responsible in any way for errors in such information provided.

First published in Japan 1993 by P·I·E BOOKS
Villa Phoenix Suite 407, 4-14-6, Komagome, Toshima-ku, Tokyo 170, Japan Tel: 03-3949-5010 Fax: 03-3949-5650
ISBN 4-938586-46-0 C3070 P16000E
First published in Germany 1993 by NIPPAN
Nippon Shuppan Hanbai Deutschland GmbH Krefelder Str.85 D-40549 Düsserdorf 11(Heerdt) Germany
Tel:0211-5048089 Fax:0211-5049326
ISBN3-910052-36-3
Printed in Japan

CONTENTS

FOREWORD / 4

POSTERS / 10

DIRECT MAILERS / 61
Invitations
Announcements
Greeting Cards
Post Cards
Tickets
Promotional Mailing

BROCHURES / 106
Pamphlets
Booklets
Leaflets
Newsletters
Flyers
Catalogues
Programmes
Annual Reports

STATIONERY / 166
Letterheads
Business Cards
Envelopes
Folders
Book Plate
Logos

PUBLICATIONS / 182
Books
Advertisements
Magazines

PACKAGING / 192
Compact Discs
Laser Disc
Video Case

CALENDARS / 195

SUBMITTOR'S INDEX / 217

1,2 & 3 COLOR Graphics

序

本書は

グラフィック・デザインの世界を色数の制限という新しい視点から捉えようというところからスタートしました。1色から3色までの限られた刷り色で効果的に表現されたグラフィックス、果たしてその様なものを集めることができるのだろうか？と多少の不安もありました。しかし世界各国から実際に私たちのもとへ応募作品が届くにつれその心配も吹き飛んでしまいました。その作品のどれもが色の少なさを感じさせない表現力に溢れ通常の4ｃ印刷にも負けない、あるいはそれ以上の魅力を持ち備えていたのです。１～３色までの限られた色数という枠のなかで構成された各作品は、ダブル・トーン、トリプル・トーンなど昔ながらの手法を最新のコンピューター処理で効果的に表現したものや、吟味された印刷色が作品をより象徴的に仕上げているもの、また、様々なインクを調合してそのデザイナー独自の色を使ったものなどそれぞれが実に多種多様なオリジナリティに富んでいます。インク会社が毎年のように発表し、限りなく増え続ける特色カラー、その中のどの色を選びそれぞれのデザインに反映させてゆくかは作り手のセンスであり、最も気を使う所でしょう。全体の作品を通して見てゆくなかで、色を少なくするということは、表現の幅を制約することではなく、むしろ作り手の想像力をよりいっそうかきたてる要素であることに気づき、デザインの持っている力を再認識しました。全てのデザイン・ワークは、クリエイターの情熱とイマジネーションによって成り立っているということを本書が証明できれば嬉しく思います。

文

1,2&3 COLOR Graphics

F O R E W

The starting point for this book was an idea we had to take a new look at the world of graphic design by limiting the number of colors that could be used. Initially we were a little uncertain whether we could gather enough material that met our criteria – we asked for submissions that used three or fewer colors and effectively conveyed a message. The submissions we received from all over the world quickly put these fears to rest. Viewing the work, we were struck by their power of expression and were never conscious of the limited number of colors in their composition. Compared to traditional four-color prints, they are not lacking in any way and in many cases are even more appealing. Working within the three-color limit, some artists have renewed traditional printing techniques like double or triple-tones by using modern computer processing to great effect, while others have taken great pains in their choice of colors, such that the printed color becomes emblematic of the work itself. Some designers have even blended inks to create their own unique colors.

The work included in this book shows a remarkable diversity and a wealth of creativity. With ink companies announcing new additions to the range of available specialty colors each year, the choice and incorporation of color by designers into their work has acquired an increasing prominence within the art of graphic design. As we looked through these pieces, we came to realize that, rather than limiting the range of expression, using fewer colors means that designers raise their creative powers to an even higher level. We were reawakened to the power of design. We sincerely hope that this volume provides ample proof of the inspiration and imaginative energy that goes into all graphic design.

O R D

1,2&3 COLOR Graphics

V O R W

Als Ausgangspunkt für dieses Buch stand die Idee, einen neuen Blickwinkel in die Welt der Grafik durch eine Einschränkung der Anzahl der zu benutzenden Farben zu gewinnen. Anfangs waren wir etwas unsicher, ob wir genug Material zusammenstellen könnten, welches unseren Maßstäben standhalten würde -- denn wir baten um Beiträge die drei oder weniger Farben verwenden, und ihre Nachricht auf effektive Weise vermitteln.. Die Beiträge die wir aus aller Welt erhielten schlichteten schnell unsere anfänglichen Befürchtungen. Beim Betrachten dieser Arbeiten waren wir von der Ausdrucksstärke beeindruckt, ohne an die geminderte Anzahl von Farben, die in den Kompositionen verwendet wurden, erinnert zu werden. Verglichen mit den üblichen Vierfarbendrucken fehlt ihnen nichts, und in manchen Fällen sind sie sogar attraktiver. Innerhalb des Bereiches von höchstens drei Farben arbeiten zu müssen, hat einige Grafiker dazu bewegt traditionelle Drucktechniken, wie den Zweifarbendruck und Dreifarbendruck, unter Anwendung von Computern mit großem Erfolg zu erneuern, während andere große Sorgfalt in der Wahl ihrer Farben bevorzugten, um somit die gedruckten Farben zu Emblemen der jeweiligen Arbeiten werden zu lassen.

Die Arbeiten in diesem Buch zeigen eine bemerkenswerte Vielfalt und einen bemerkenswerten Reichtum an Kreativität auf. Mit den alljährlichen Mitteilungen der Farbindustrien über die neuen Variationen innerhalb der Serien der Spezialfarben, nimmt die Wahl und Miteinbezugsnahme von Farbtönen in der grafischen Arbeit eine prominente und wachsende Stellung ein. Bei der Ansicht der vorliegenden Werke stellten wir fest, daß anstatt die Ausdrucksmöglichkeiten einzuschränken, der Gebrauch von weniger Farben die Kreativität der Designer in ein höheres Niveau verlegte. Wir entdeckten in gewissem Sinne auch die Stärke der Gestaltung wieder. Wir hoffen sehr, daß dieser Band die Inspiration und Vorstellungskraft, die in jeder grafischen Arbeit vorhanden ist, zur Genüge belegt.

O R T

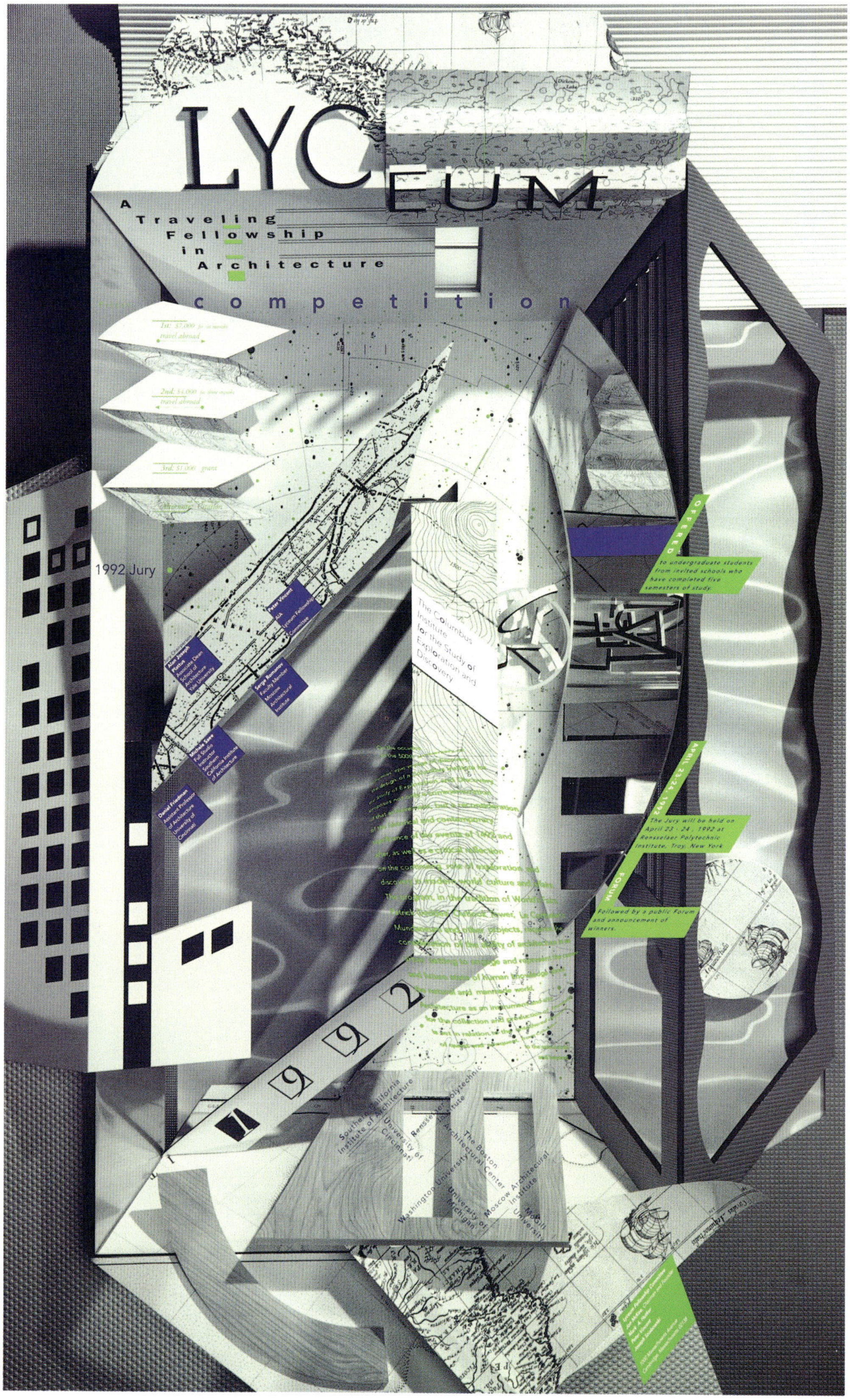
LYCEUM
A Traveling Fellowship in Architecture
competition
1st: $7,000 travel abroad
2nd: $4,000 travel abroad
3rd: $1,000 grant
1992 Jury
The Columbus Institute for the Study of Exploration and Discovery
OFFERED
to undergraduate students from invited schools who have completed five semesters of study.
The Jury will be held on April 22 - 24, 1992 at Rensselaer Polytechnic Institute, Troy, New York
Followed by a public Forum and announcement of winners.
1992

CD: Nancy Skolos and Thomas Wedell D: Nancy Skolos P: Thomas Wedell DF: Skolos / Wedell CL: Lyceum Fellowship Committee USA 1991

architects language

CD, AD, D, I: Peter Grundy DF: Peter Grundy Ownworks CL: Peter Grundy England 1993

petergrundy nworks
15
100

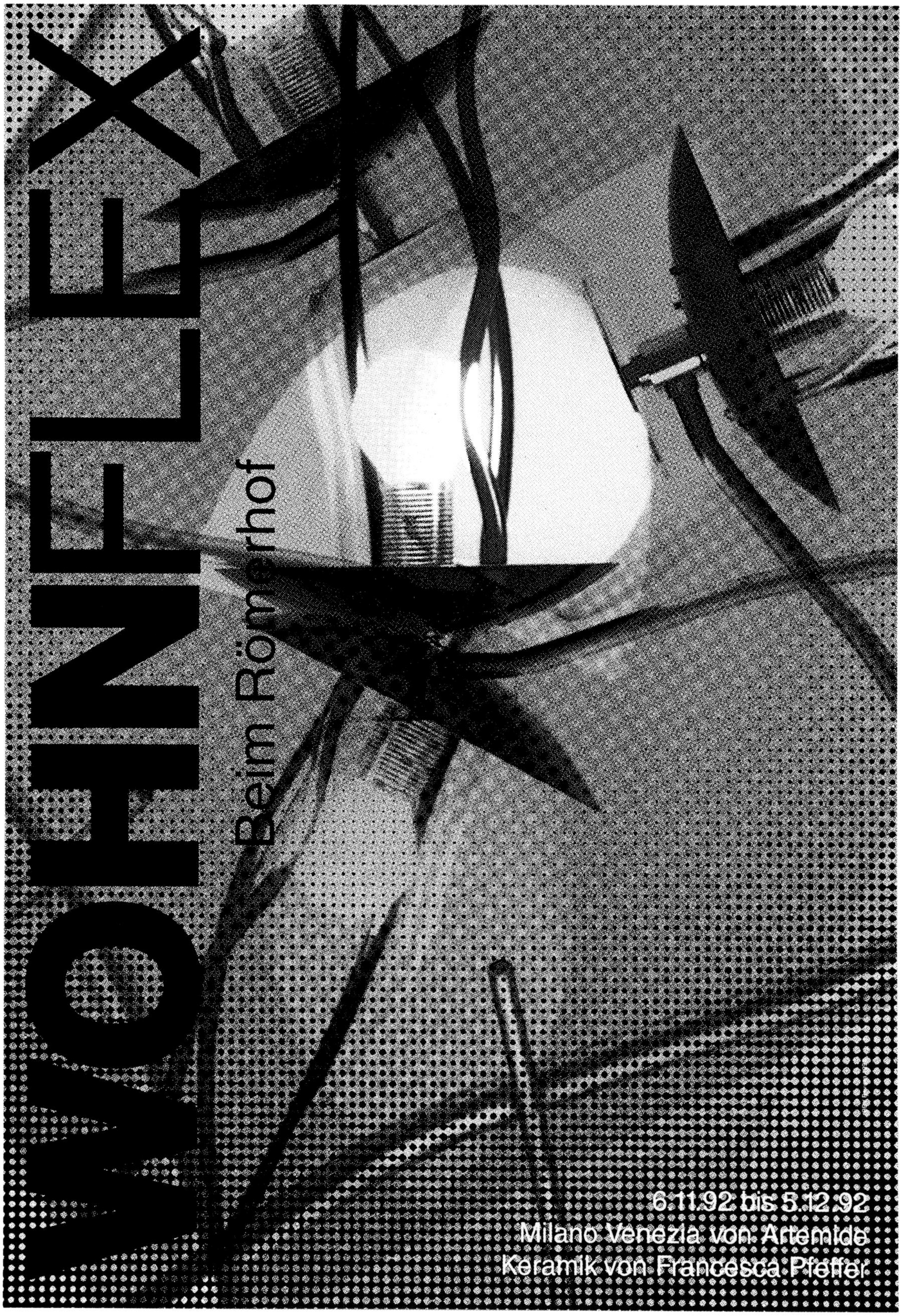

CD, AD, D: Michael Baviera D: Anke Felgenhauer DF: BBV CL: Wohnflex Switzerland 1992

CD, AD, D, P, CW: Tadeusz Piechura DF: Atelier Tadeusz Piechura CL: General Director Zdzislaw Hejduk Poland 1990

AD, D: Simon Sernec CW: Roman Brilej CL: ZGRAF 6 Slovenia 1991

CD, I: Akemi Suetsugu AD, D: Katsunori Aoki CL: Akemi Suetsugu Japan 1993

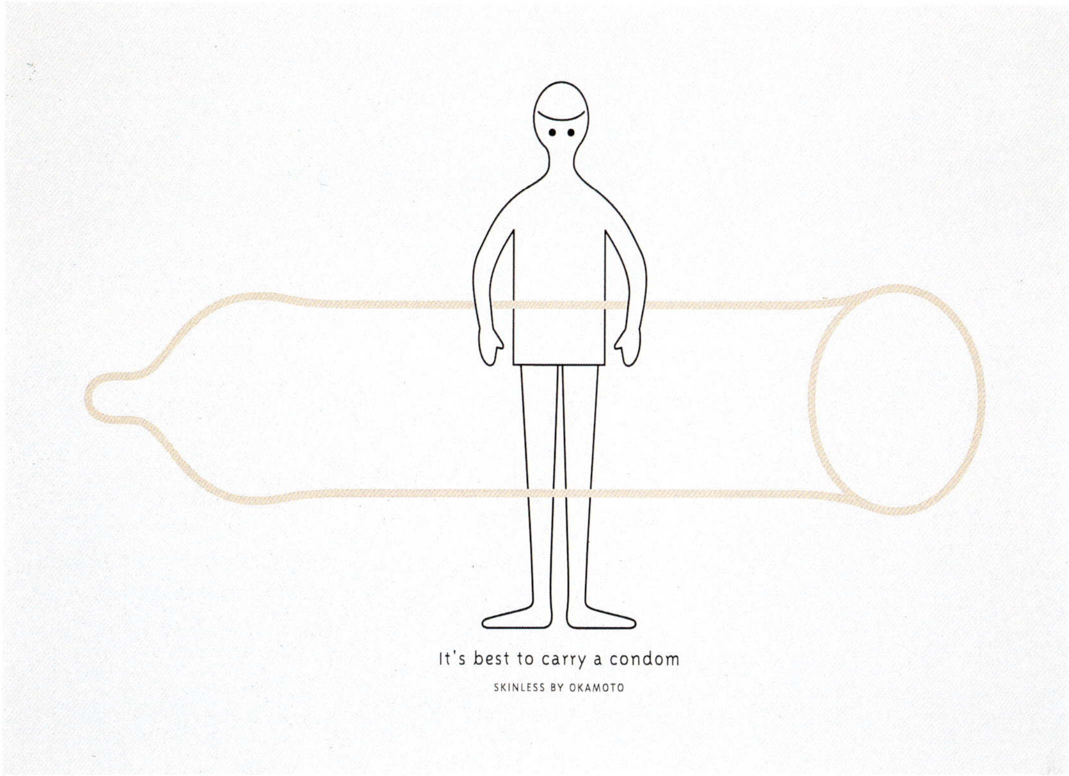

CD: Kenji Hanaue AD, D, I: Katsunori Aoki DF: Dentsu PR Center CL: Okamoto Japan 1993

T MB

AD, D, I: Thomas Marutschke CL: Edition Spinetti & Wagner Germany 1992

V

CD, AD, D: André Baldinger CW: ANCT CL: ANCT France 1993

AD: Rebeca Mendez D: Darin Beaman & Rebeca Mendez P: Steven A. Heller / Tarsem
DF: Art Center College of Design - Design Office CL: Art Center College of Design USA 1993

D: Willi Kunz P: Skyviews DF: Willi Kunz Associates CL: Columbia University USA 1980

F
F

AD, D: Clifford Stoltze P: Anton Grassl DF: Clifford Stoltze Design CL: AIGA Boston USA 1993

CD, AD, D: Art Chantry P: Arthur S. Aubry CL: Sub Pop USA 1992

CD, AD, D: Art Chantry CL: New City Theater USA 1985

CD, AD, D: Art Chantry CL: Organic Theatre Company USA 1990

CD, AD, D: Bill Gardner / Sonia Greteman DF: Gardner + Greteman CL: AIGA Midwest USA 1992

CD, AD, D: Art Chantry CL: KZOK USA 1991

CD, AD, D: John Spatchurst P: F. Adriani DF: Spatchurst Design Associates CL: Art Gallery of New South Wales Australia 1990

CD, AD, D, P, I, CW: Robert Bergman-Ungar CL: Janou Pakter USA 1992

CD, AD, D: Katsunori Aoki CD: Youdai Sadamura AD,D: David Duval Smith AD: Yoshimi Aoba CL: moo moo connection Japan 1993

D: Rudy Vanderlans DF: Emigre Graphics CL: Emigre Music USA 1990

F

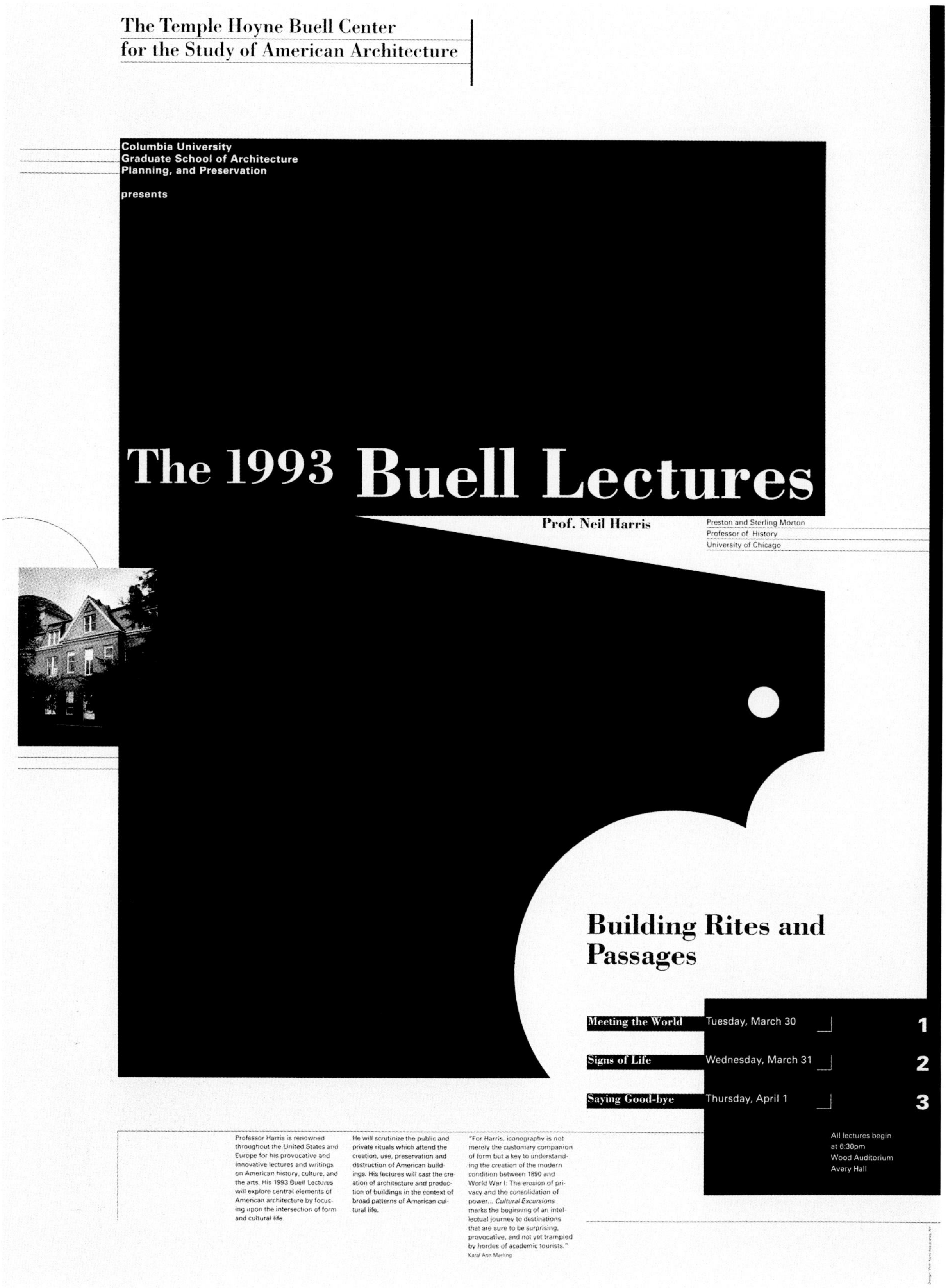

D: Willi Kunz P: Fredrich Cantor DF: Willi Kunz Associates CL: Columbia University USA 1993

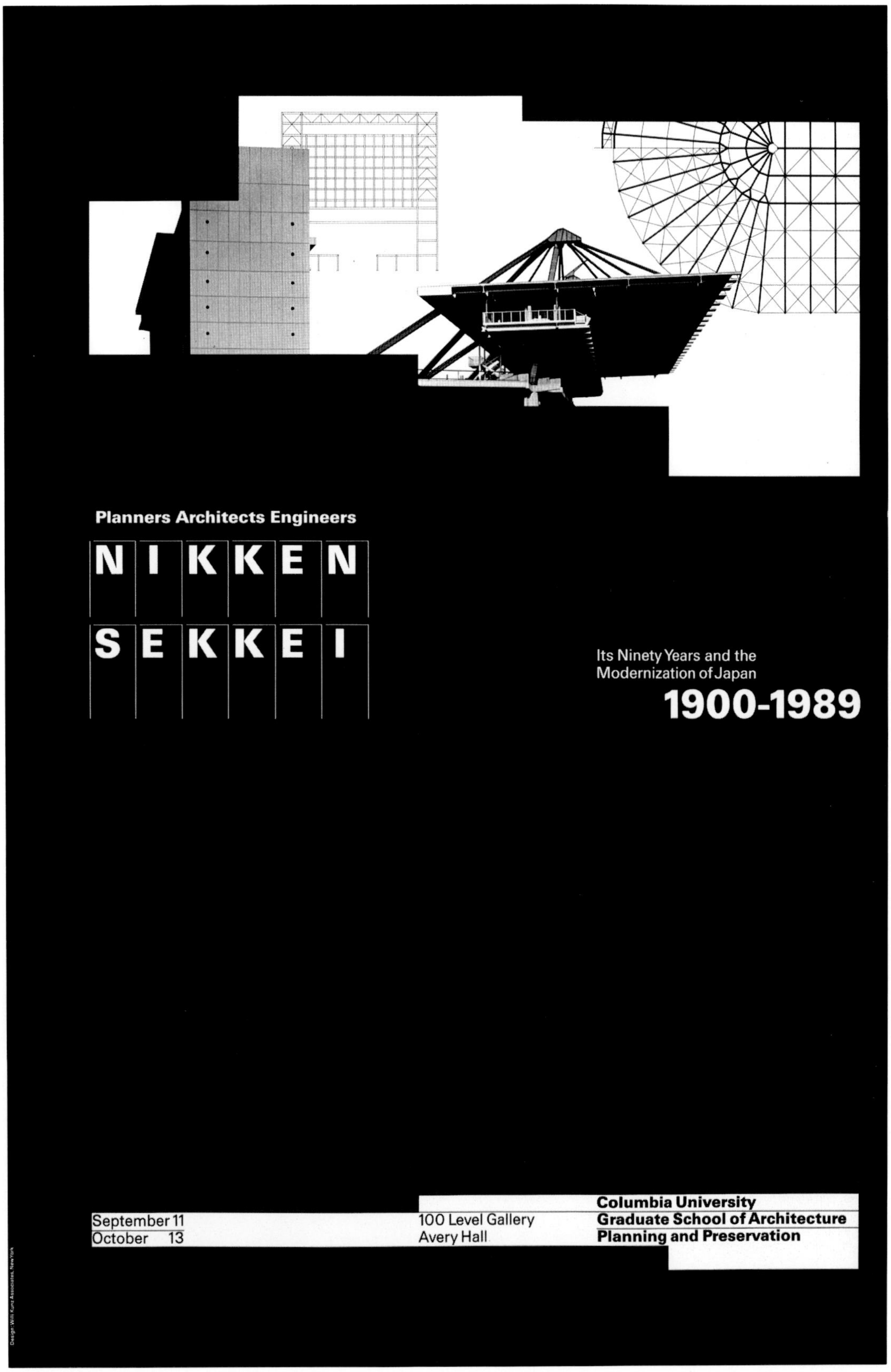

D: Willi Kunz DF: Willi Kunz Associates CL: Nikken Sekkei USA 1989

AD, I: Kunio Hikita CL: Hikita World Japan 1993

I: Kunio Hikita CL: Hikita World Japan 1993

AD: Gento Matsumoto DF: Saru Brunei CL: Studio Ambient Japan 1992

CD, D: Nancy Skolos CD, P: Thomas Wedell DF: Skolos / Wedell CL: Lyceum Fellowship Committee USA 1993

CD, D: Nancy Skolos CD, P: Thomas Wedell DF: Skolos / Wedell CL: WHDV Channel 7 USA 1991

AD, D: Ichiro Mitani P: Gakuji Tanaka DF: Mitani Ichiro Design Studio CL: Sumitomo 3M Japan 1991

CD, AD, D, P, I, CW: Robert Bergman-Ungar CL: Jodi Rappaport USA 1992

AD, D: Masaaki Hiromura D: Nobuhiko Aizawa DF: Hiromura Design Office CL: Parco Japan 1992

CD: Junzo Ogawa AD, D: Masayuki Shimizu CW: Kyoko Mikazuki DF: Heter-O-Doxy Protprast CL: Aids Bowl Associate Japan 1993

G

AD, D: Masaaki Hiromura D: Toshiyuki Kojima DF: Hiromura Design Office CL: The Yurakucho Seibu Japan 1993

AD, D: Masaaki Hiromura D: Nobuhiko Aizawa DF: Hiromura Design Office CL: Komagane Kogen Art Museum Japan 1993

D, P: Elisabeth Charman Typeface Designer: Frank Heine DF: Emigre Graphics CL: Emigre Fonts USA 1993

AD, D, I: Karin Neumert CL: Kulturamt Rüsselsheim Germany 1993

AD, D, I: Karin Neumert CL: Asta Kulturreferat Mainz Germany 1992

D, I: Mark Fox DF, CL: BlackDog USA 1991

CD, AD, D, I: Hans-Rudolf Lutz / Marc Philipp DF: Lutz CL: Schweizerischer Gewerkschaftsbund Switzerland 1992

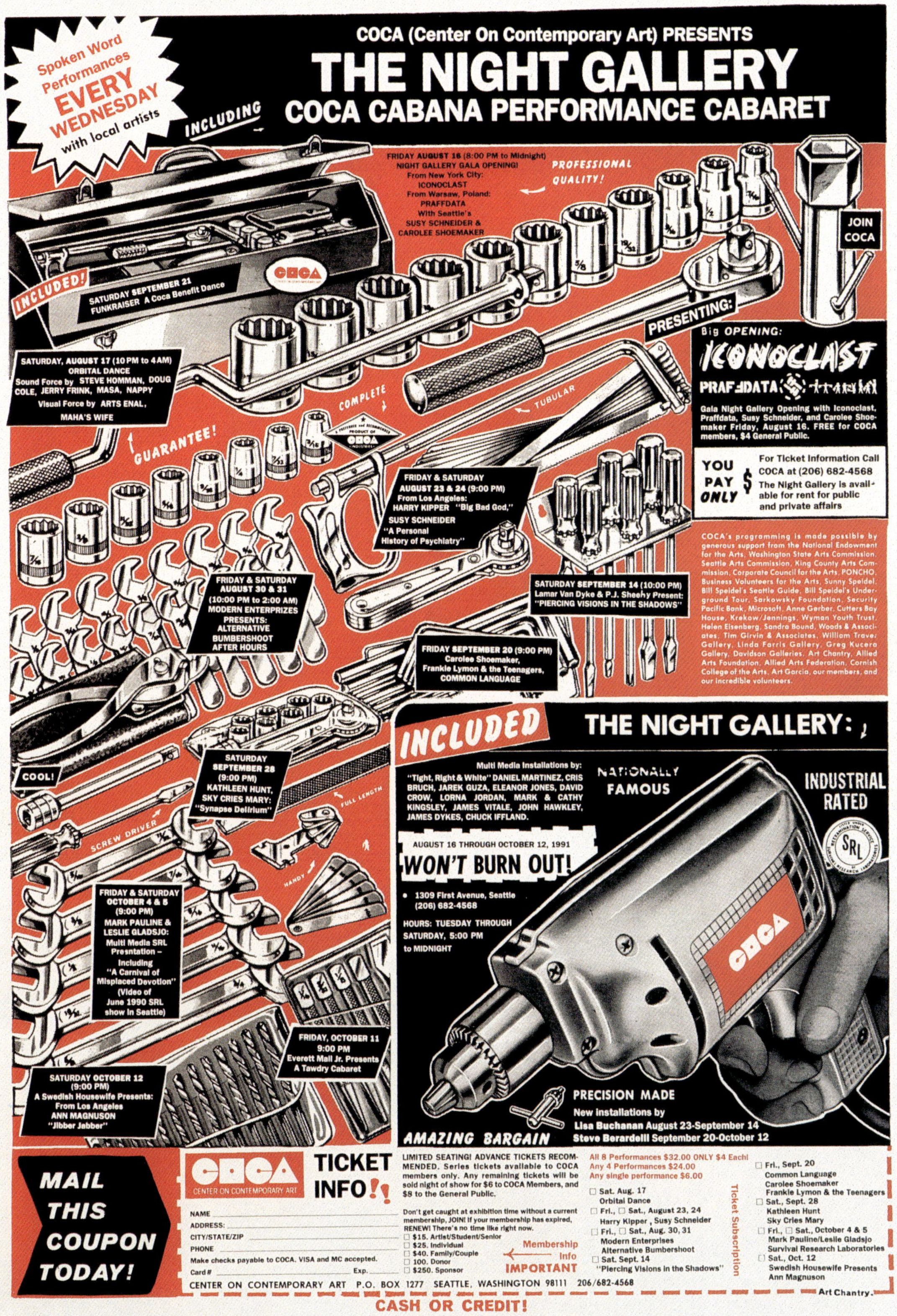
Spoken Word Performances EVERY WEDNESDAY with local artists
INCLUDING
COCA (Center On Contemporary Art) PRESENTS
THE NIGHT GALLERY
COCA CABANA PERFORMANCE CABARET
FRIDAY AUGUST 16 (8:00 PM to Midnight) NIGHT GALLERY GALA OPENING! From New York City: ICONOCLAST From Warsaw, Poland: PRAFFDATA With Seattle's SUSY SCHNEIDER & CAROLEE SHOEMAKER
PROFESSIONAL QUALITY!
JOIN COCA
INCLUDED!
SATURDAY SEPTEMBER 21 FUNKRAISER A Coca Benefit Dance
PRESENTING:
SATURDAY, AUGUST 17 (10 PM to 4 AM) ORBITAL DANCE Sound Force by STEVE HOMMAN, DOUG COLE, JERRY FRINK, MASA, NAPPY Visual Force by ARTS ENAL, MAHA'S WIFE
COMPLETE
TUBULAR
GUARANTEE!
Big OPENING:
ICONOCLAST
PRAFFDATA
Gala Night Gallery Opening with Iconoclast, Praffdata, Susy Schneider, and Carolee Shoemaker Friday, August 16. FREE for COCA members, $4 General Public.
YOU PAY ONLY $
For Ticket Information Call COCA at (206) 682-4568
The Night Gallery is available for rent for public and private affairs
FRIDAY & SATURDAY AUGUST 23 & 24 (9:00 PM) From Los Angeles: HARRY KIPPER "Big Bad God," SUSY SCHNEIDER "A Personal History of Psychiatry"
FRIDAY & SATURDAY AUGUST 30 & 31 (10:00 PM to 2:00 AM) MODERN ENTERPRIZES PRESENTS: ALTERNATIVE BUMBERSHOOT AFTER HOURS
SATURDAY SEPTEMBER 14 (10:00 PM) Lamar Van Dyke & P.J. Sheehy Present: "PIERCING VISIONS IN THE SHADOWS"
COCA's programming is made possible by generous support from the National Endowment for the Arts, Washington State Arts Commission, Seattle Arts Commission, King County Arts Commission, Corporate Council for the Arts, PONCHO, Business Volunteers for the Arts, Sunny Speidel, Bill Speidel's Seattle Guide, Bill Speidel's Underground Tour, Sarkowsky Foundation, Security Pacific Bank, Microsoft, Anne Gerber, Cutters Bay House, Krekow/Jennings, Wyman Youth Trust, Helen Eisenberg, Sandra Bound, Woods & Associates, Tim Girvin & Associates, William Traver Gallery, Linda Farris Gallery, Greg Kucera Gallery, Davidson Galleries, Art Chantry, Allied Arts Foundation, Allied Arts Federation, Cornish College of the Arts, Art Garcia, our members, and our incredible volunteers.
FRIDAY SEPTEMBER 20 (9:00 PM) Carolee Shoemaker, Frankie Lymon & the Teenagers, COMMON LANGUAGE
INCLUDED
THE NIGHT GALLERY:
COOL!
SATURDAY SEPTEMBER 28 (9:00 PM) KATHLEEN HUNT, SKY CRIES MARY: "Synapse Delirium"
FULL LENGTH
SCREW DRIVER
HANDY
Multi Media Installations by: "Tight, Right & White" DANIEL MARTINEZ, CRIS BRUCH, JAREK GUZA, ELEANOR JONES, DAVID CROW, LORNA JORDAN, MARK & CATHY KINGSLEY, JAMES VITALE, JOHN HAWKLEY, JAMES DYKES, CHUCK IFFLAND.
NATIONALLY FAMOUS
INDUSTRIAL RATED
SRL
AUGUST 16 THROUGH OCTOBER 12, 1991
WON'T BURN OUT!
1309 First Avenue, Seattle (206) 682-4568
HOURS: TUESDAY THROUGH SATURDAY, 5:00 PM to MIDNIGHT
FRIDAY & SATURDAY OCTOBER 4 & 5 (9:00 PM) MARK PAULINE & LESLIE GLADSJO: Multi Media SRL Presntation – Including "A Carnival of Misplaced Devotion" (Video of June 1990 SRL show in Seattle)
COCA
FRIDAY, OCTOBER 11 9:00 PM Everett Mall Jr. Presents A Tawdry Cabaret
SATURDAY OCTOBER 12 (9:00 PM) A Swedish Housewife Presents: From Los Angeles ANN MAGNUSON "Jibber Jabber"
PRECISION MADE
New installations by
Lisa Buchanan August 23-September 14
Steve Berardelli September 20-October 12
AMAZING BARGAIN
MAIL THIS COUPON TODAY!
COCA CENTER ON CONTEMPORARY ART
TICKET INFO!!
LIMITED SEATING! ADVANCE TICKETS RECOMMENDED. Series tickets available to COCA members only. Any remaining tickets will be sold night of show for $6 to COCA Members, and $8 to the General Public.
NAME
ADDRESS:
CITY/STATE/ZIP
PHONE
Make checks payable to COCA. VISA and MC accepted.
Card # Exp.
Don't get caught at exhibition time without a current membership, JOIN! If your membership has expired, RENEW! There's no time like right now.
☐ $15. Artist/Student/Senior
☐ $25. Individual
☐ $40. Family/Couple
☐ 100. Donor
☐ $250. Sponsor
Membership Info IMPORTANT
All 8 Performances $32.00 ONLY $4 Each!
Any 4 Performances $24.00
Any single performance $6.00
☐ Sat. Aug. 17 Orbital Dance
☐ Fri., ☐ Sat., August 23, 24 Harry Kipper, Susy Schneider
☐ Fri., ☐ Sat., Aug. 30, 31 Modern Enterprises Alternative Bumbershoot
☐ Sat. Sept. 14 "Piercing Visions in the Shadows"
Ticket Subscription
☐ Fri., Sept. 20 Common Language Carolee Shoemaker Frankie Lymon & the Teenagers
☐ Sat., Sept. 28 Kathleen Hunt Sky Cries Mary
☐ Fri., ☐ Sat., October 4 & 5 Mark Pauline/Leslie Gladsjo Survival Research Laboratories
☐ Sat., Oct. 12 Swedish Housewife Presents Ann Magnuson
CENTER ON CONTEMPORARY ART P.O. BOX 1277 SEATTLE, WASHINGTON 98111 206/682-4568
Art Chantry.
CASH OR CREDIT!

MB

AD, D, I: Kenzo Izutani DF: Kenzo Izutani Office CL: Parco Japan 1992

CD: Fumikazu Masuda AD: Kenzo Kobayashi D: Hideo Ogino P: Toshiro Takayama
CW: Tadashi Konno DF: Kenzo Kobayashi Design CL: Okamura Japan 1989

AD, D: Edi Berk P: Tone Stojko DF: KROG CL: GL (Town Theatre of Ljubljana) Slovenia 1991-1992

CD, AD: Katsu Asano D: Kinue Yonezawa P: Taka Kobayashi DF: ASA 100 Company CL: Barreaux Division Scoop Japan 1992

CD, AD, D: Art Chantry CL: Unexpected Productions USA 1991

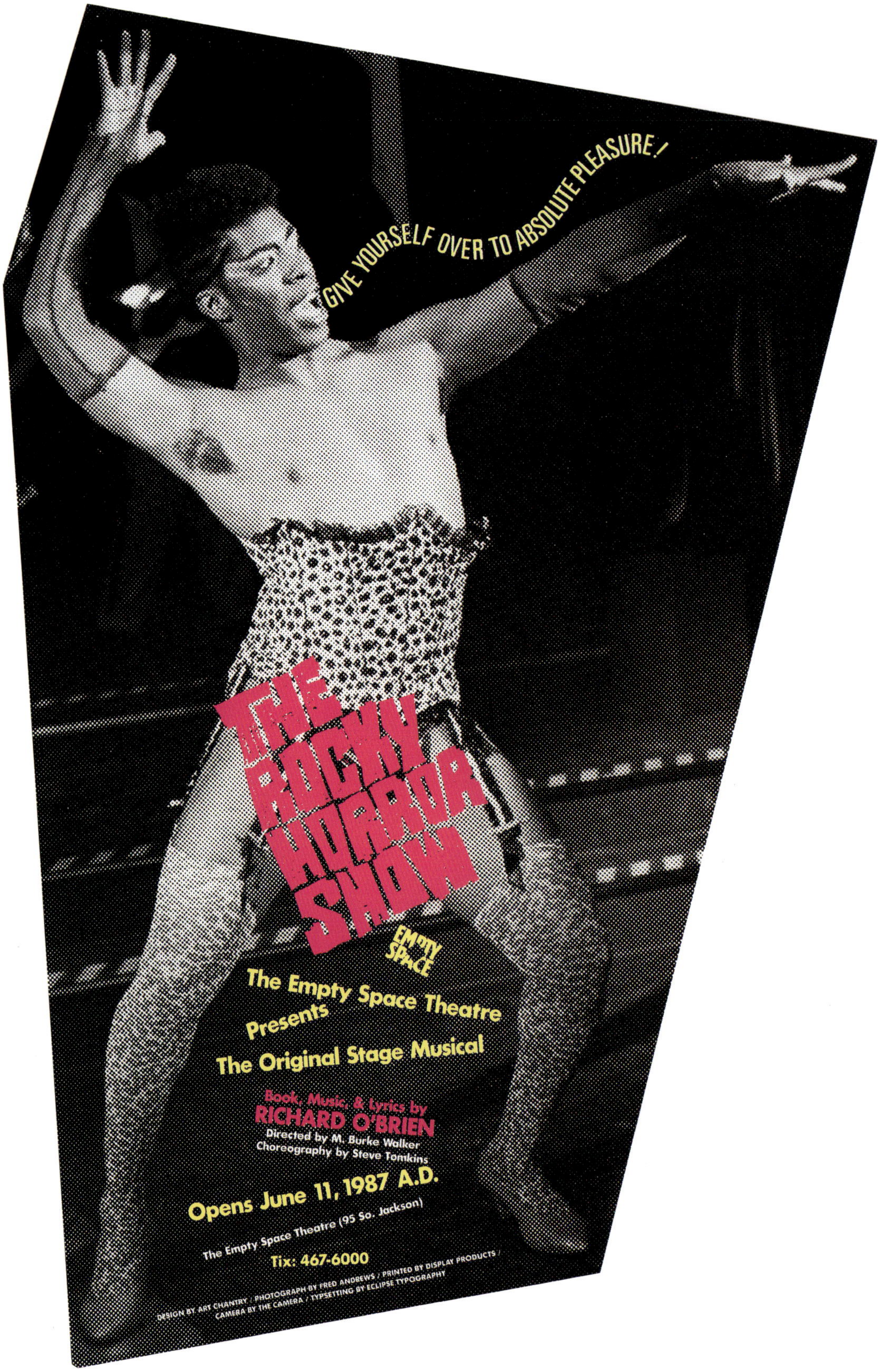

F F

CD, AD, D: Art Chantry P: Fred Andrews CL: Empty Space USA 1987

AD: Mark Timmings D: Mario Godbout CW: Philippe Sigouin / Richard Lebel DF: Turquoise Design CL: Turquoise Design Canada 1992-1993

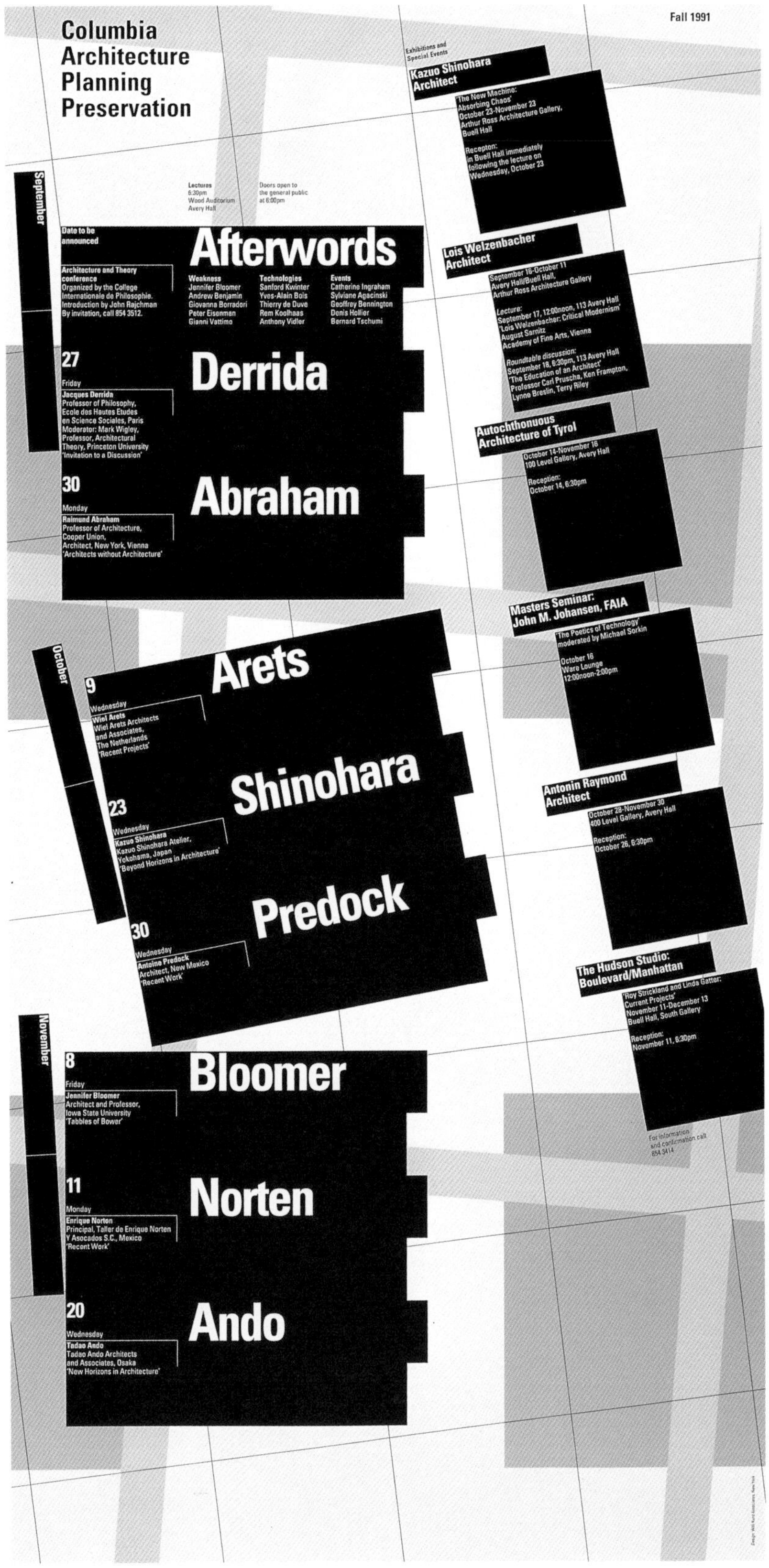

D: Willi Kunz DF: Willi Kunz Associates CL: Columbia University USA 1991

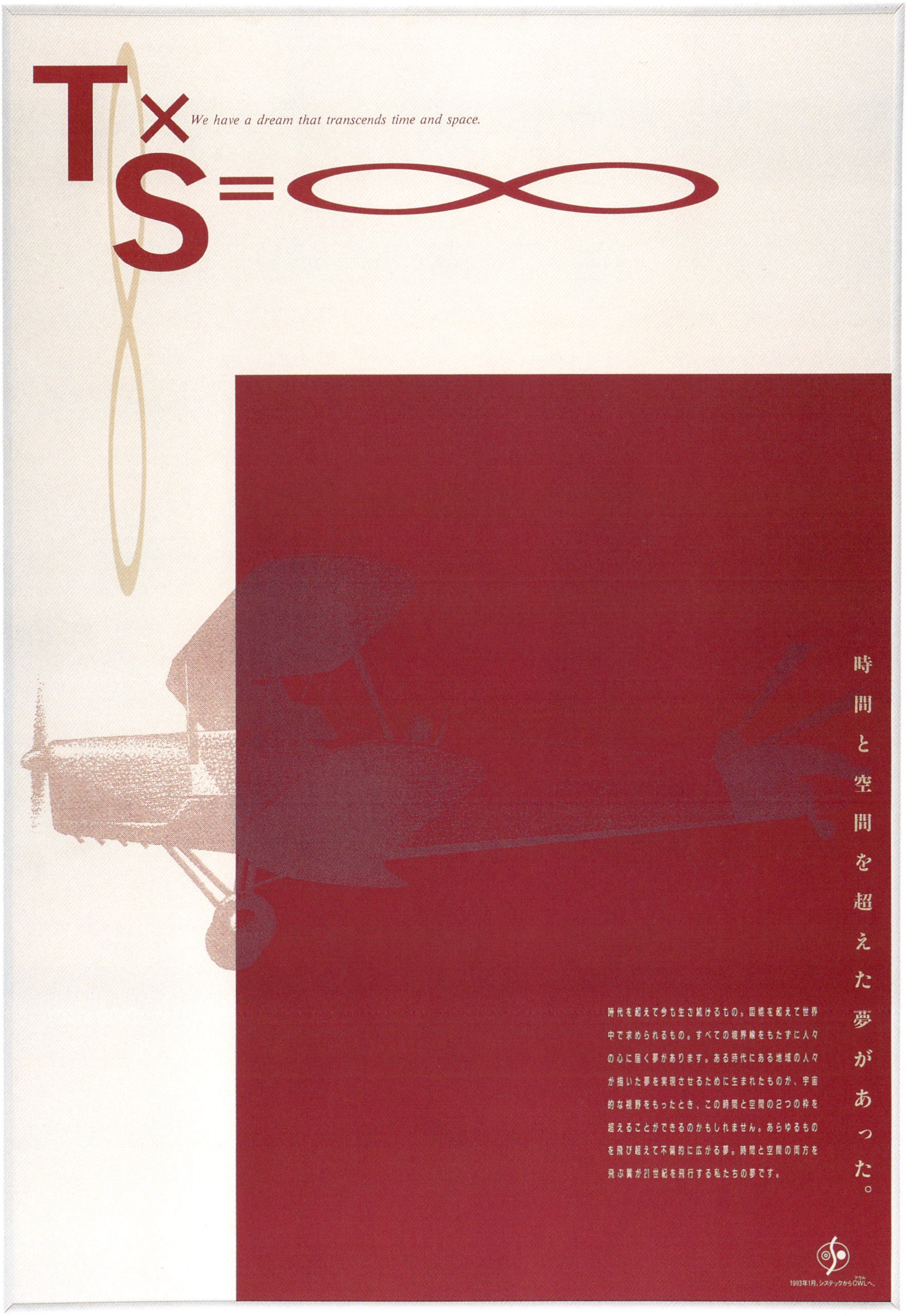

CD: Minekazu Kazawa AD: Kozo Takahata D: Yasunori Nodamura CW: Noriko Suzaki DF: AD·Able CL: OWL Japan 1992

M

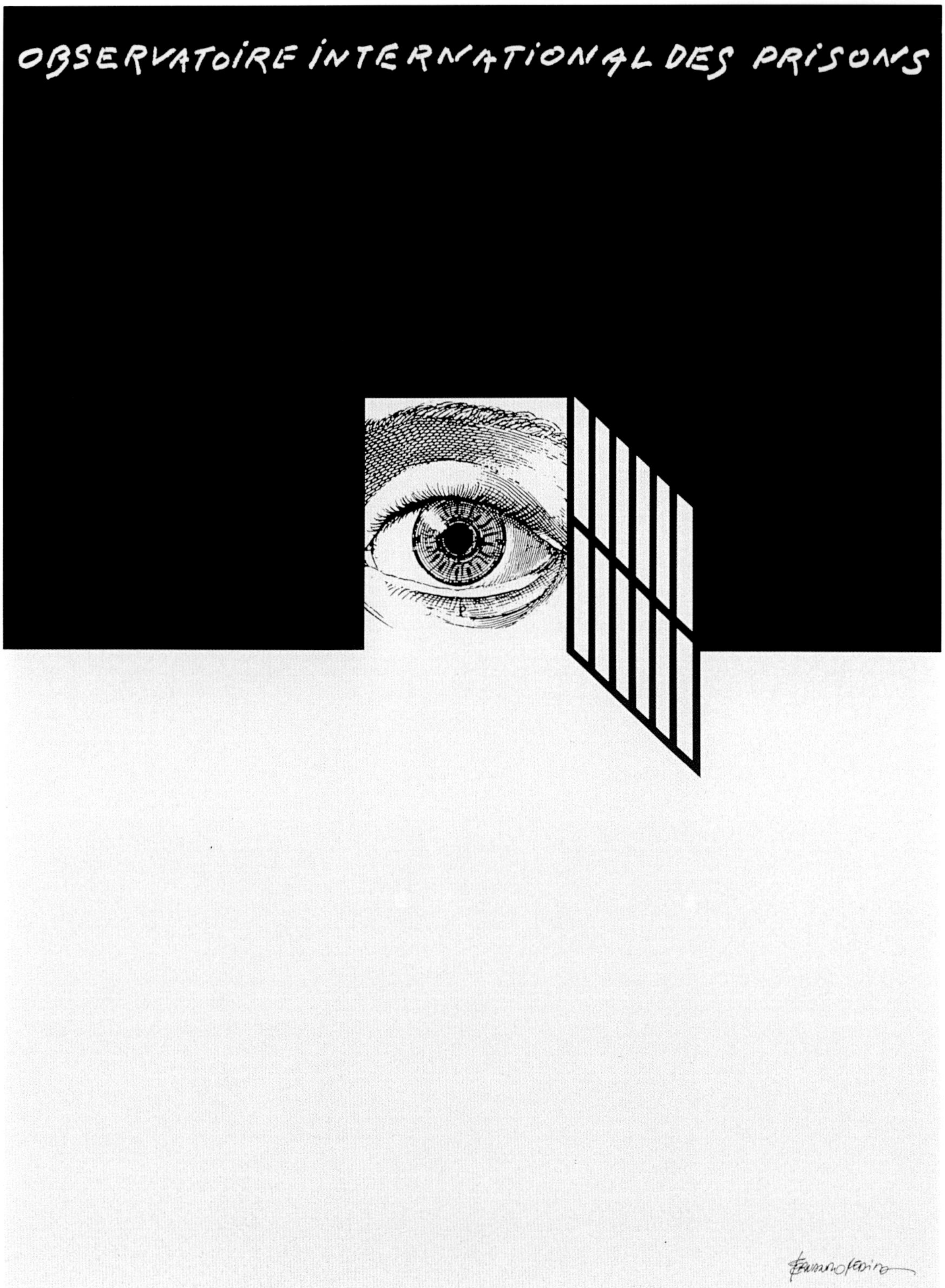

AD, D, I: Fernando Medina DF: Triom Design CL: OIDP France USA 1993

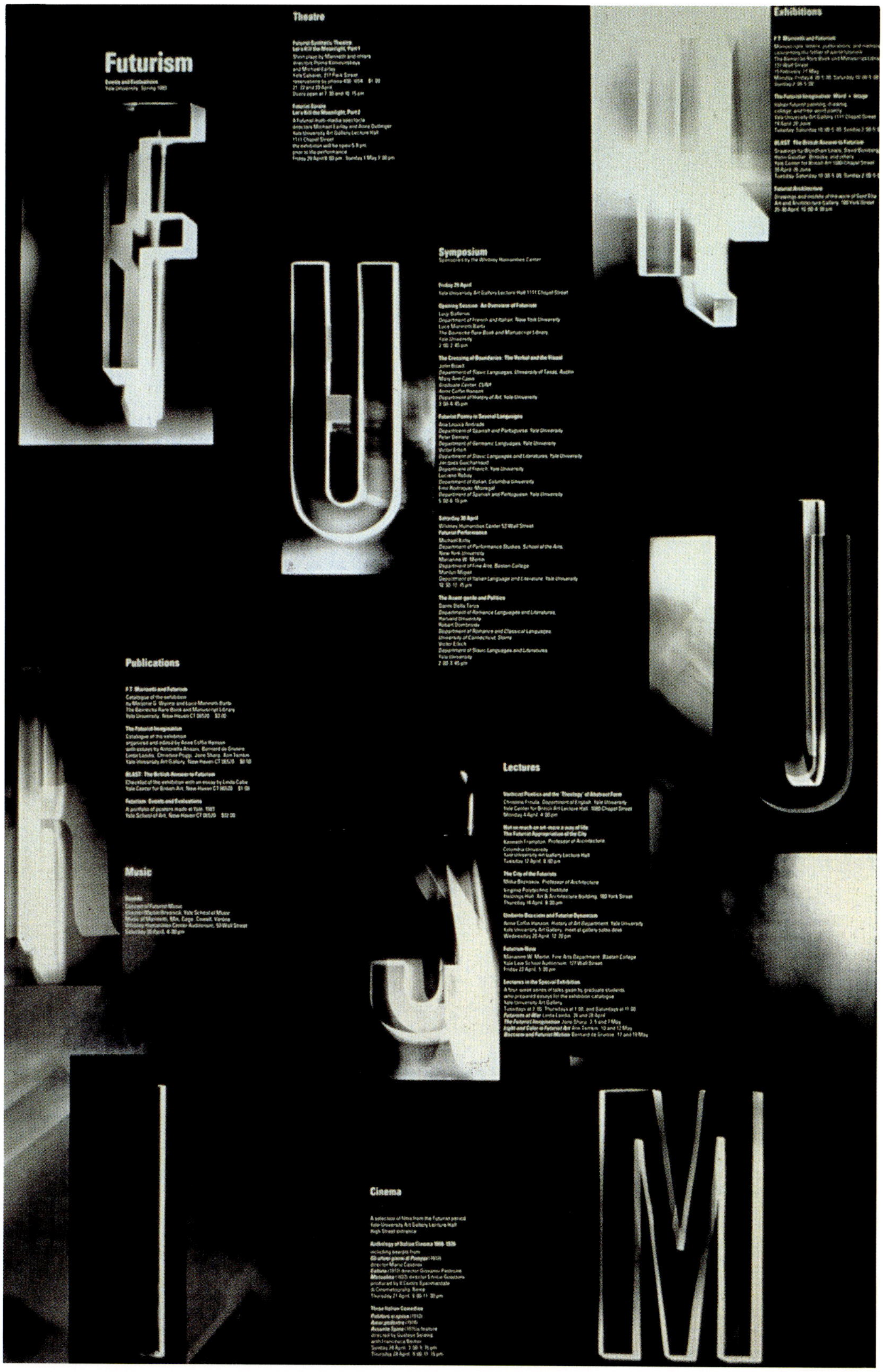

D, P: Ramona Hutko DF: Ramona Hutko Design CL: Yale University USA 1988

CD: Masaru Okamoto D: Hiroe Mizuno CL: Dai-ichi Hotel Tokyo Bay Japan 1992

AD, D, I: Shuzo Kato DF: Kato Shuzo Design Product CL: Chubu Creators Club Japan 1992

CD, AD, D, I: John Sayles DF: Sayles Graphic Design CL: Iowa-Nebraska Farm Equipment Association USA 1991

CD, AD, D: Michael Baviera DF: BBV CL: Museum Baviera Switzerland 1991

AD: José Serrano D, I: Tracy Sabin DF: Mires Design CL: Bordeaux Printers USA 1992

AD: Lisa Porter I: Tracy Sabin DF: Design Safari CL: Icarus Studio USA 1992

AD, D, I: Steven Guarnaccia CL: Val d'Orbieu Wines USA 1991-1992

CD: Esther Smith / Dikko Faust I: Melinda Beck CL: Purgatory Pie Press USA 1992

D, I: Steven Guarnaccia CL: Steven Guarnaccia USA 1990

AD: Dikko Faust / Esther K. Smith D, I: Steven Guarnaccia CL: Purgatory Pie Press USA 1989

CD, AD, D, I: Carlos Segura DF: Segura CL: Gimcracks USA 1992

1.

2.

3.

CD, AD, I: Lanny Sommese D: Kristin Sommese DF: Sommese Design CL: Sommese Design USA 1992 1.

CD, AD, D, CW: Kristin Sommese AD, I: Lanny Sommese DF: Sommese Design CL: Sommese Design USA 1990 2.

CD, AD, D, I: Lanny Sommese DF: Sommese Design CL: Dante's Restaurants USA 1987 3.

CD: Esther Smith / Dikko Faust I: Melinda Beck CL: Purgatory Pie Press USA 1992

CD, AD, D, I: Romane Cameron DF: Studio Seireeni CL: Studio Seireeni USA 1992

CD: Junko Wong AD, D, I: Isabelle Dervaux CL: CWC USA 1992

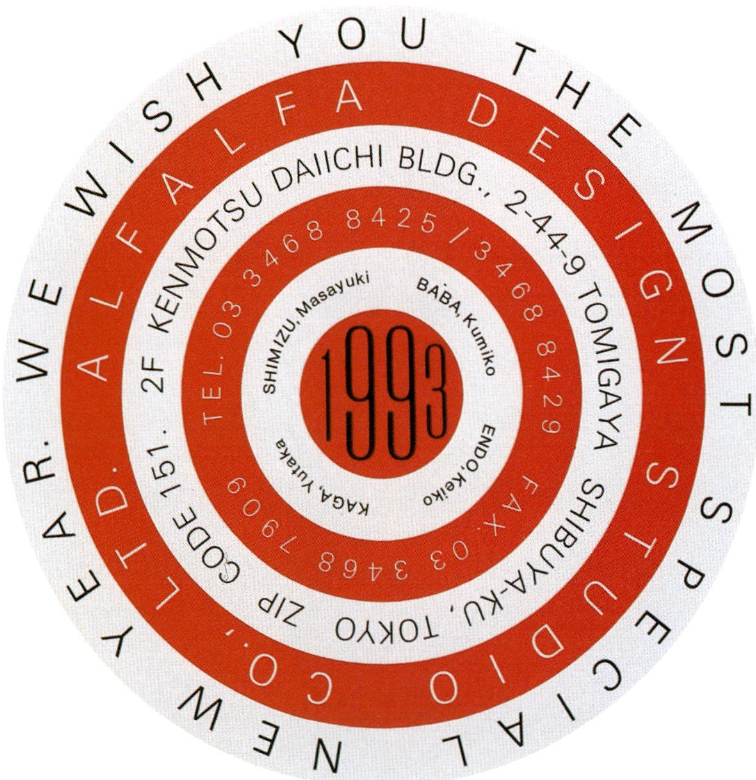

AD, D: Kumiko Baba CL: Alfalfa Design Studio Japan 1993

CD, AD, D: Takaaki Matsumoto CD, AD: Michael McGinn DF: M Plus M CL: The Southall Group USA 1991

D, I: Yuichi Nakagawa DF: Kinema Moon designing CL: Kinema Moon designing Japan 1990

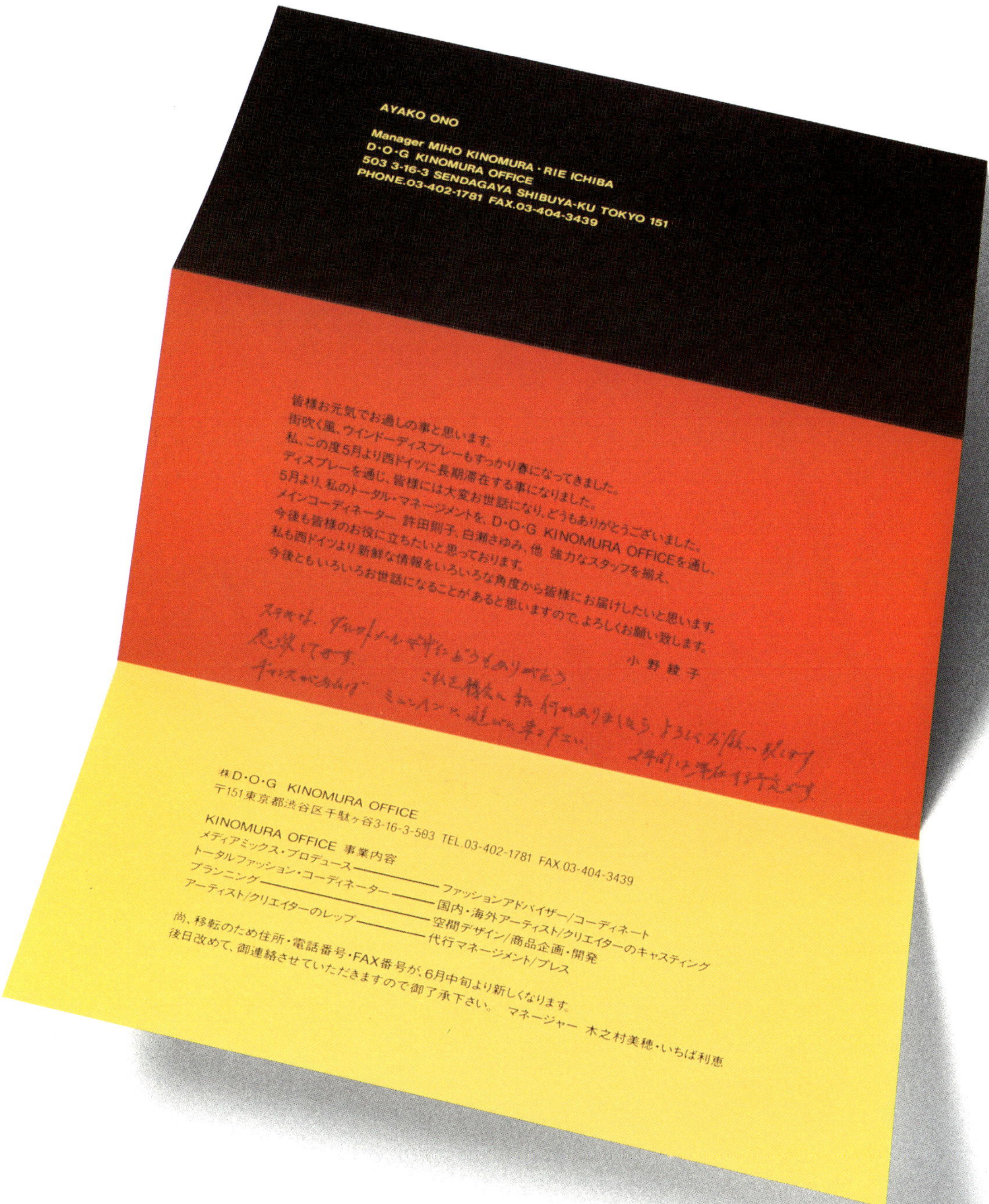

CD, AD, D: Keisuke Unosawa DF: Keisuke Unosawa Design CL: Ayako Ono Japan 1988

CD, AD, D: Michael McGinn DF: M Plus M CL: Independent Curators USA 1987

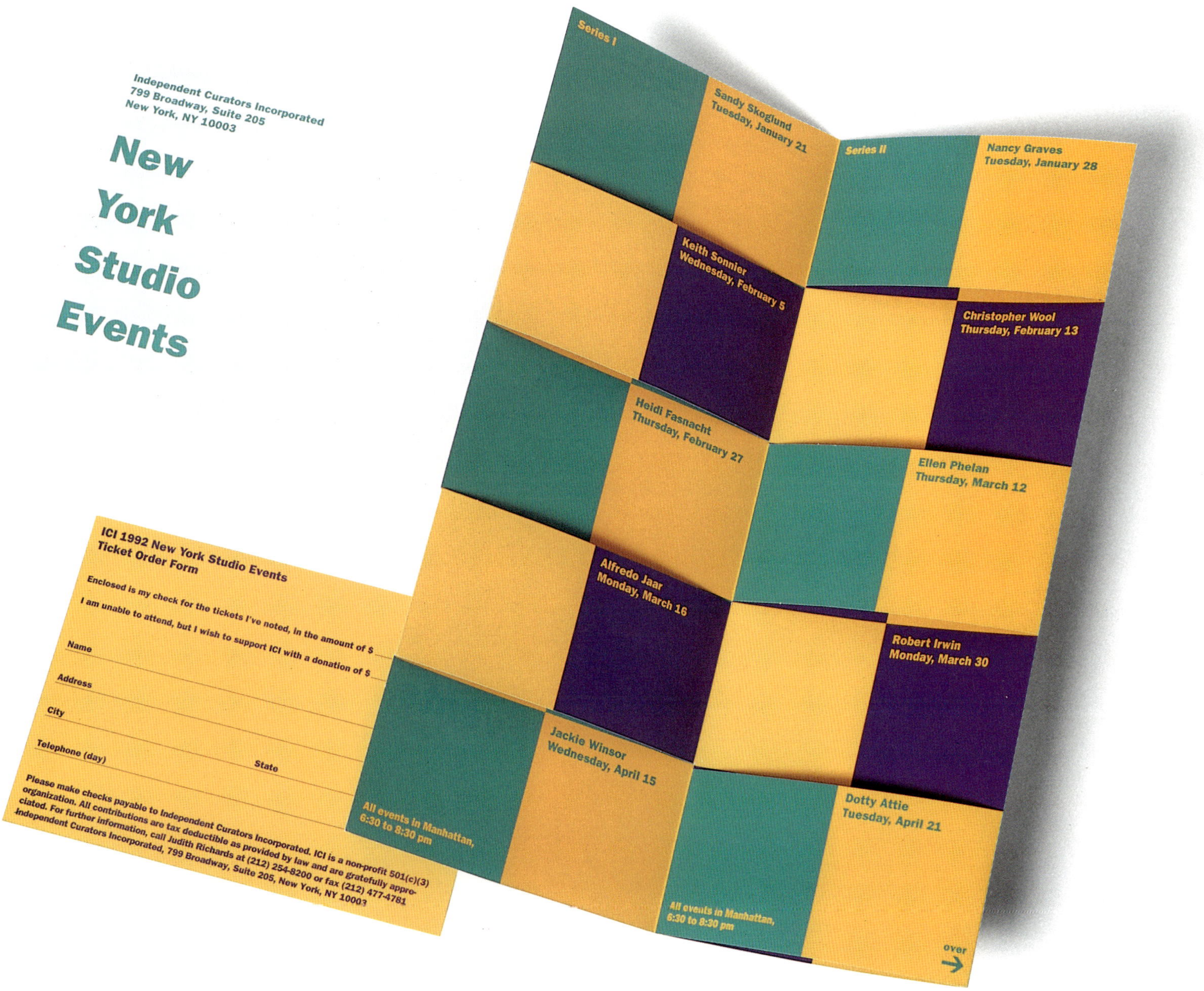
Independent Curators Incorporated
799 Broadway, Suite 205
New York, NY 10003
New York Studio Events
ICI 1992 New York Studio Events
Ticket Order Form
Enclosed is my check for the tickets I've noted, in the amount of $
I am unable to attend, but I wish to support ICI with a donation of $
Name
Address
City
Telephone (day)
State
Please make checks payable to Independent Curators Incorporated. ICI is a non-profit 501(c)(3) organization. All contributions are tax deductible as provided by law and are gratefully appreciated. For further information, call Judith Richards at (212) 254-8200 or fax (212) 477-4781
Independent Curators Incorporated, 799 Broadway, Suite 205, New York, NY 10003
Series I
Sandy Skoglund
Tuesday, January 21
Series II
Nancy Graves
Tuesday, January 28
Keith Sonnier
Wednesday, February 5
Christopher Wool
Thursday, February 13
Heidi Fasnacht
Thursday, February 27
Ellen Phelan
Thursday, March 12
Alfredo Jaar
Monday, March 16
Robert Irwin
Monday, March 30
Jackie Winsor
Wednesday, April 15
Dotty Attie
Tuesday, April 21
All events in Manhattan,
6:30 to 8:30 pm
All events in Manhattan,
6:30 to 8:30 pm
over

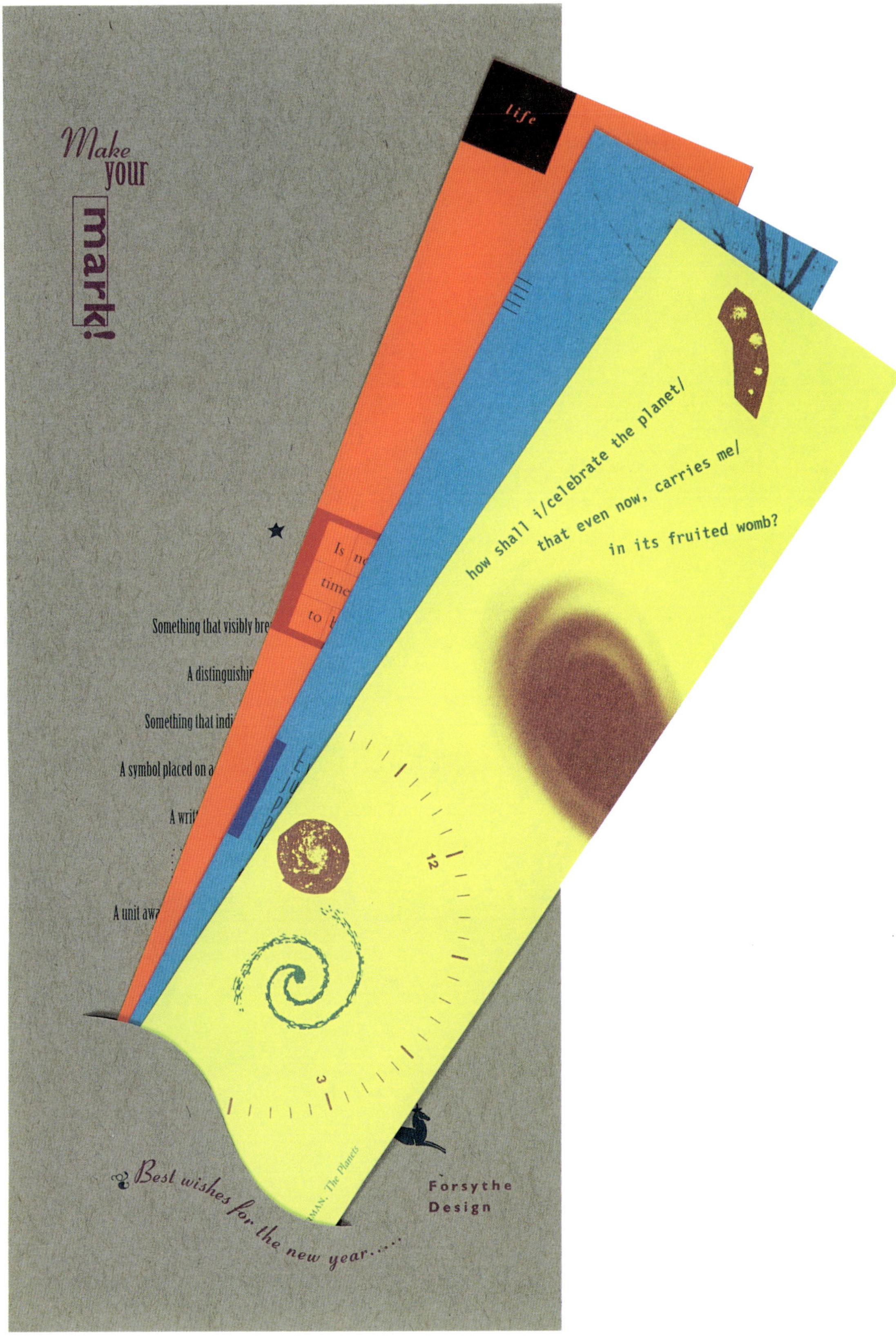
Make your mark!
life
Something that visibly bre
A distinguishi
Something that indi
A symbol placed on a
A unit awa
how shall i/celebrate the planet/
that even now, carries me/
in its fruited womb?
12
3
Best wishes for the new year.....
Forsythe Design

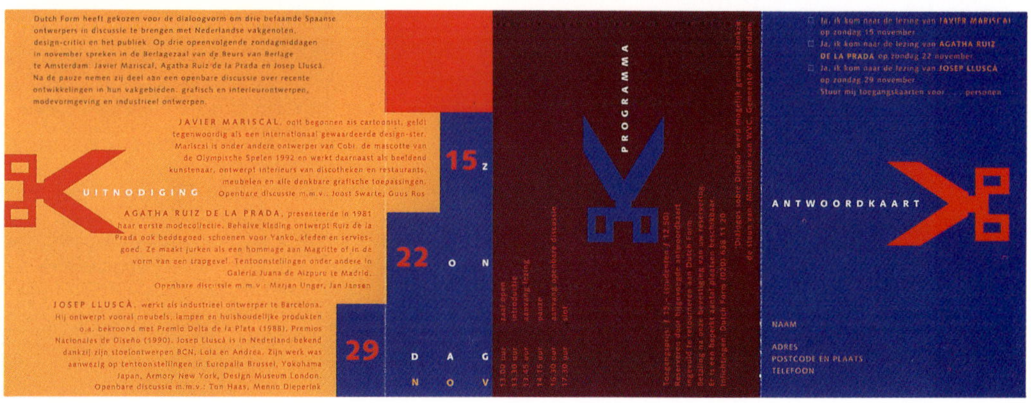

CD, AD, D: Keisuke Unosawa DF: Keisuke Unosawa Design CL: D·O·G International Japan 1990

CD, D, I: Montse Hernández Sala CL: Dutch Form (Amsterdam) The Netherlands 1992

CD, AD: John Rushworth AD, D: Vince Frost P: The Douglas Brothers DF: Pentagram Design CL: Art and Architecture England 1992-1993

CD, AD: John Rushworth AD, D: Vince Frost DF: Pentagram Design CL: Art and Architecture England 1992-1993

AD, D: Kumiko Baba CL: Alfalfa Design Studio Japan 1992

G

CD, AD, D: Richard Seireeni P: Mathew Rolston DF: Studio Seireeni CL: Studio Seireeni USA 1990

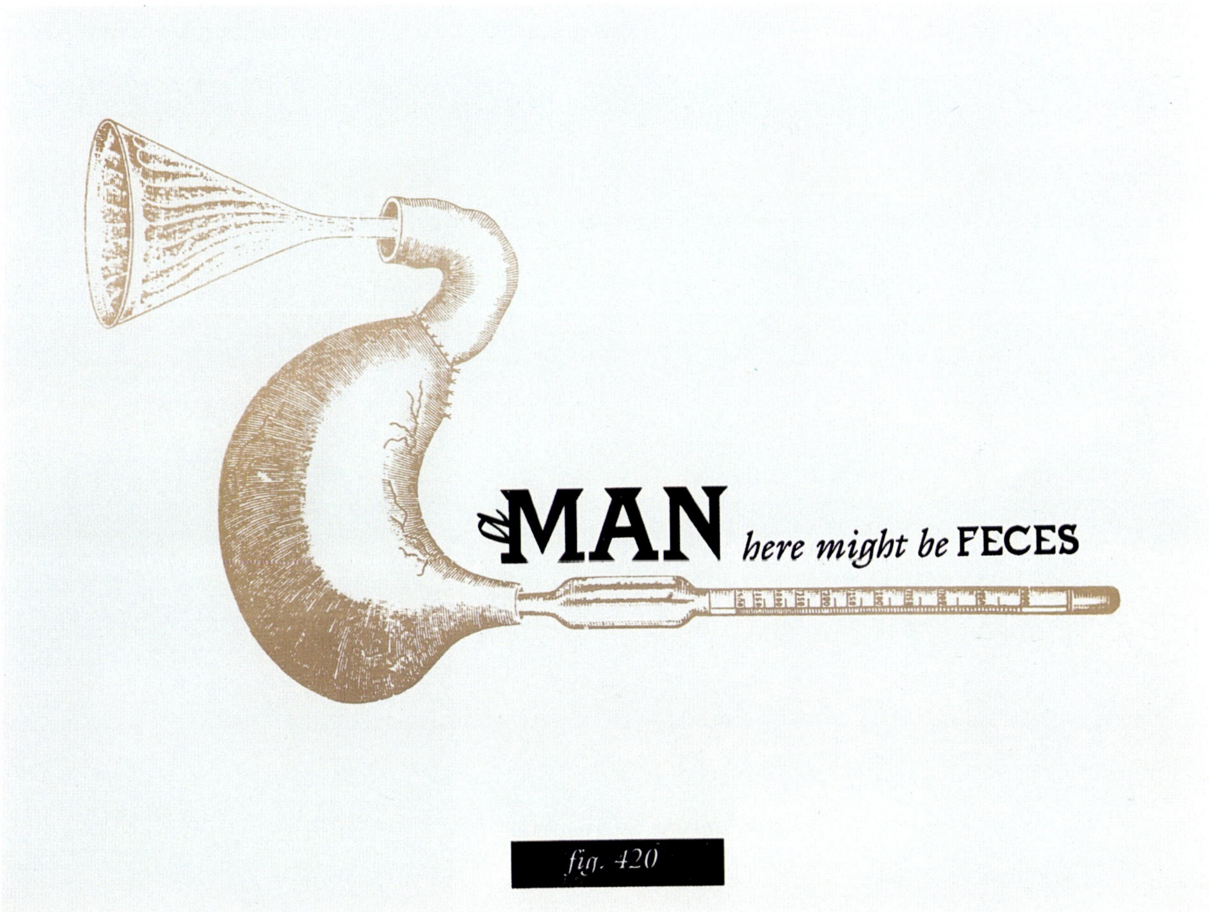

D, P: Brian Smith CL: Brian Smith USA 1993

D: Brian Schorn DF: Cranbrook Academy of Art, Department of Design CL: Brian Schorn USA 1992

D: Akihiko Tsukamoto CL: B.B.C. Japan 1987

AD, D: Hiroshi Seki P: Masao Murabayashi CL: Shadow Photos Japan 1993

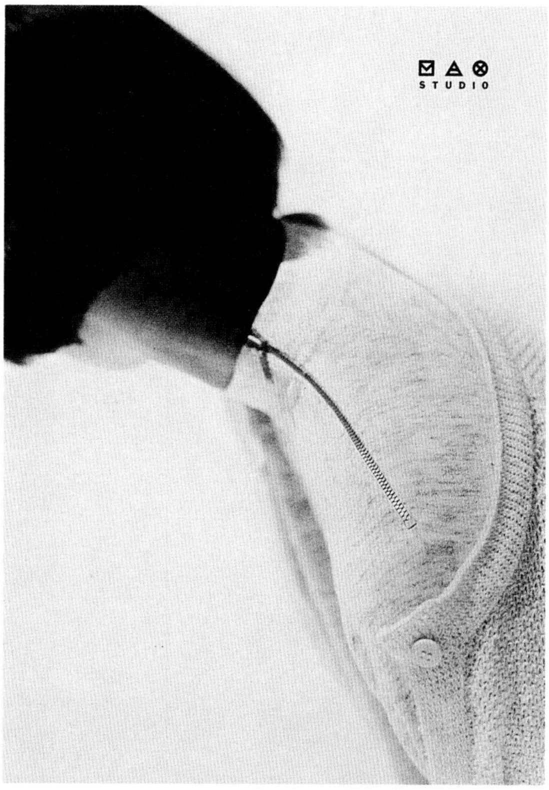

1.

2.

3.

CD, AD, D: Richard Seireeni P: Phillip Dixon DF: Vigon Seireeni CL: Leon Max USA 1986 1.

AD, D: Hisao Sugiura P: Thierry Chomel / Yutaka Yamamoto D, DF: Studio Super Compass CL: Yohji Yamamoto Japan 1993 2.

CD, AD, D: Richard Seireeni P: Phillip Dixon DF: Vigon Seireeni CL: Leon Max USA 1986 3.

CD, AD, D: David Hurren / Ian Hutchings DF: Two CL: Pepe Jeans / Lynne Franks P.R. England 1992

AD: Bob Manley D, I: Steven Guarnaccia D: Brent Croxton DF: Trout CL: Kendall Square Research USA 1991

CD, AD, D, CW: Marc Lochs CL: Marc Lochs The Netherlands 1993

AD, D: Aad van Dommelen D: Ciaran O'Goara / Marc van der Heyde DF: Proforma Rotterdam, Association for Design & Consult
CL: Utrecht University The Netherlands 1992-1993

D: Fred Bower CL: Detroit Artist Market USA 1992

D, P: Brian Smith CL: Cranbrook Academy of Art Museum USA 1992

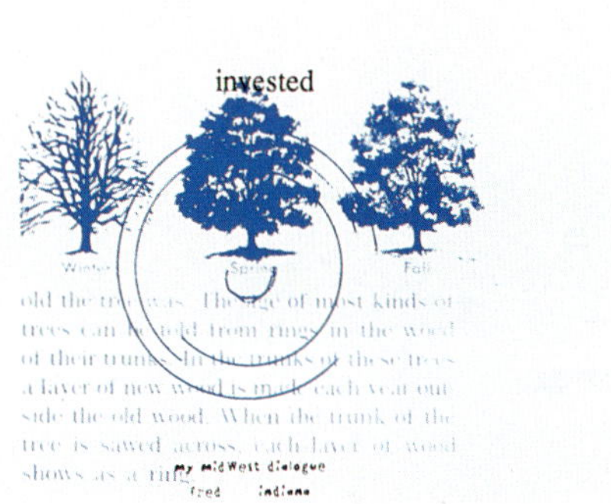

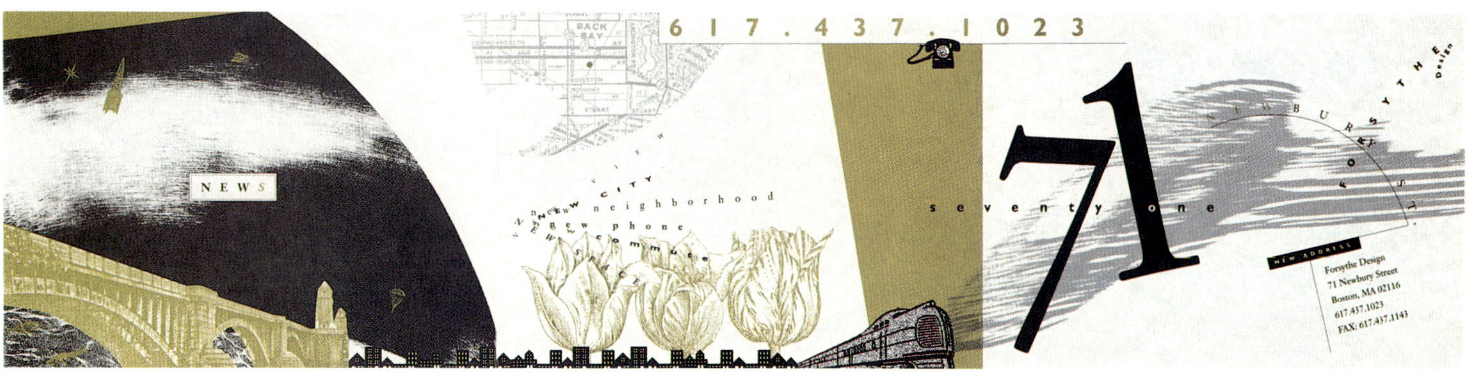

CD: Kathy McCoy D: Fred Bower CL: Kathy McCoy USA 1993

AD: Kathy Forsythe D, P: Jane Cuthbertson DF: Forsythe Design CL: Forsythe Design USA 1991

AD, DF: Michael Stanard D: Lisa Fingerhut CL: Northlight Theatre USA 1992

CD, AD, D: Bill Gardner / Sonia Greteman AD, D: Karen Hogan DF: Gardner + Greteman CL: Wichita Chamber of Commerce USA 1992

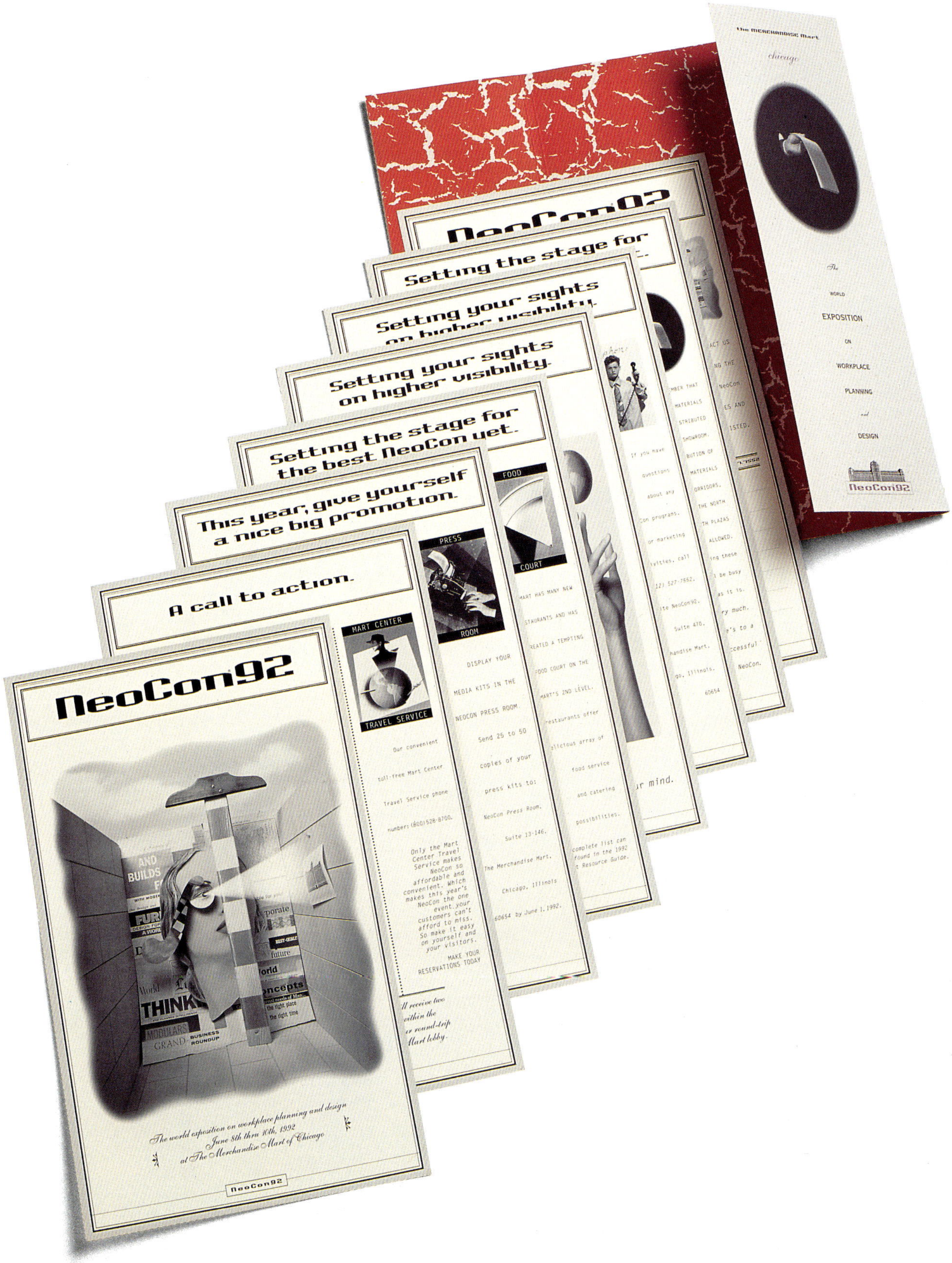

CD, AD, D: Carlos Segura P: Geof Kern DF: Segura CL: The Merchandise Mart USA 1992

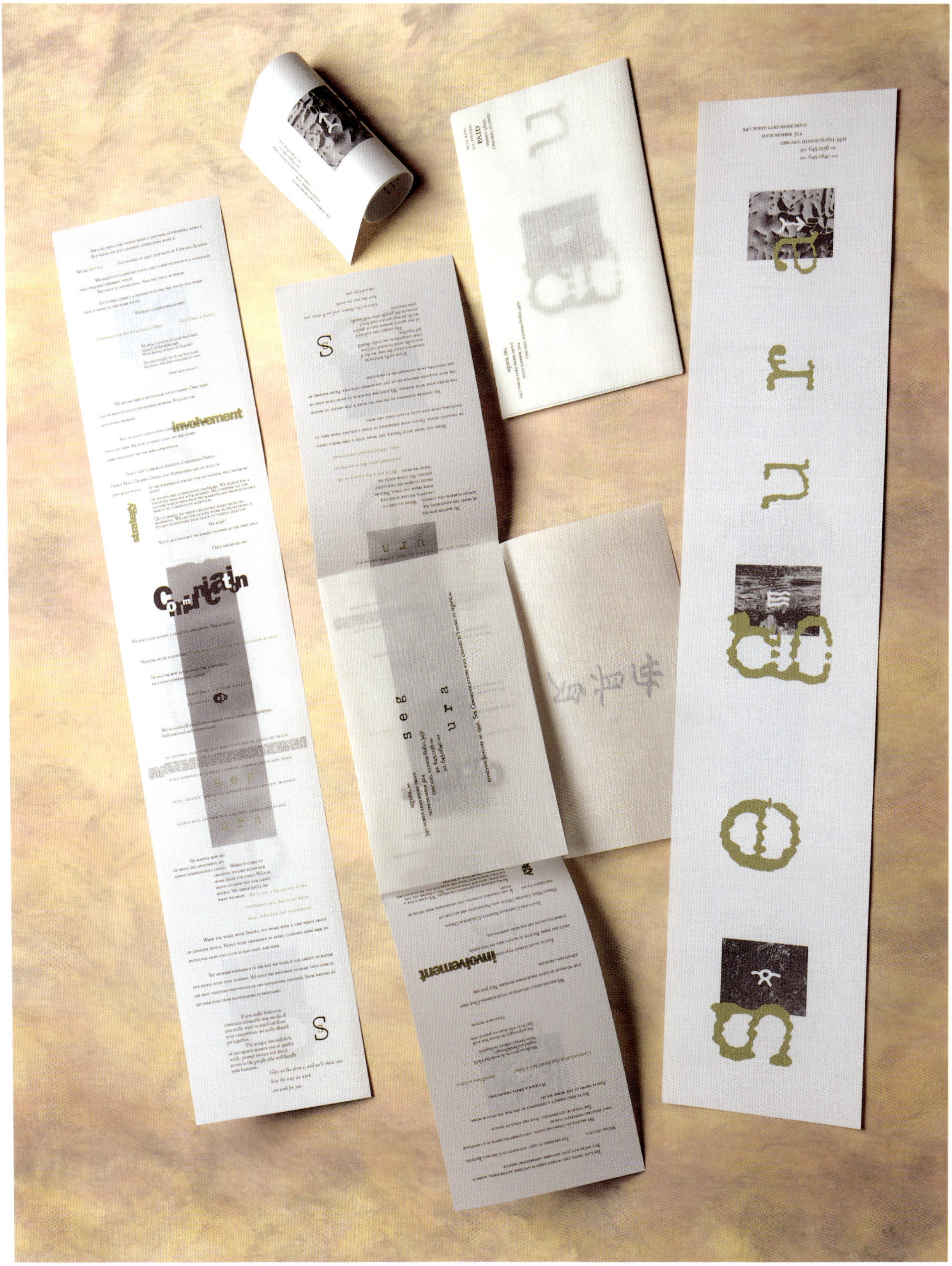

CD, AD, D: Carlos Segura P: Steve Nozicka DF: Segura CL: Segura USA 1992

D: Brenda Rotheiser DF: Cranbrook Academy of Art, Department of Design CL: Cranbrook Academy of Art USA 1992

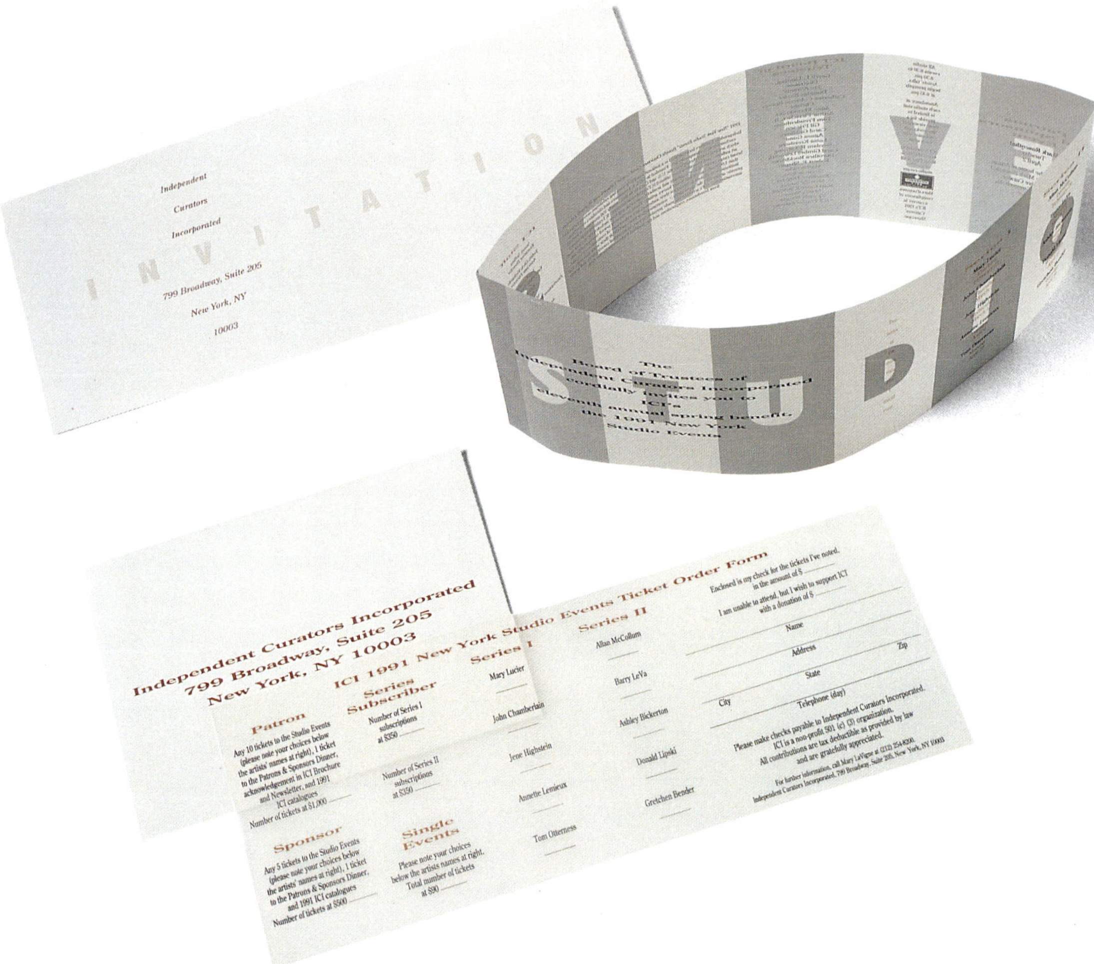

S C

CD, AD, D: Michael McGinn CD, AD: Takaaki Matsumoto DF: M Plus M CL: Independent Curators USA 1990

CD, AD, D: Kristin Sommese CD, AD, I: Lanny Sommese DF: Sommese Design CL: Lanny & Kristin Sommese USA 1991

AD, D: Stefanie Choi CL: Michele Vivona & Keith Heffernan USA 1992

AD, D: Margo Sepanski CW: Jan Chow CL: Jan Chow USA 1990

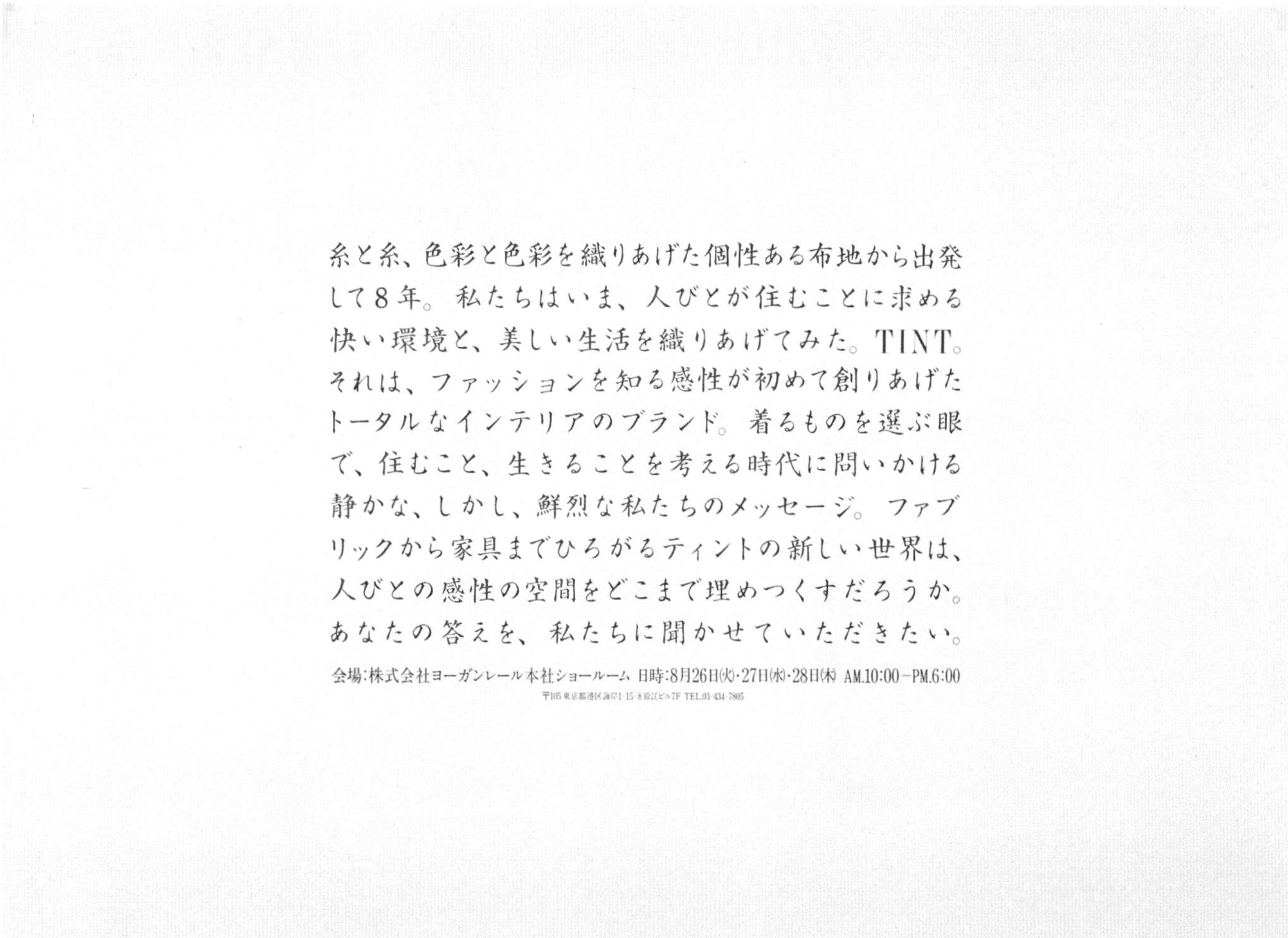

AD: Akira Inada D: Akihiko Tsukamoto CW: Shigeri Kurisu CL: Jurgen Lehl Japan 1984

AD: Mikio Ioka DF: elephant CL: elephant Japan 1991

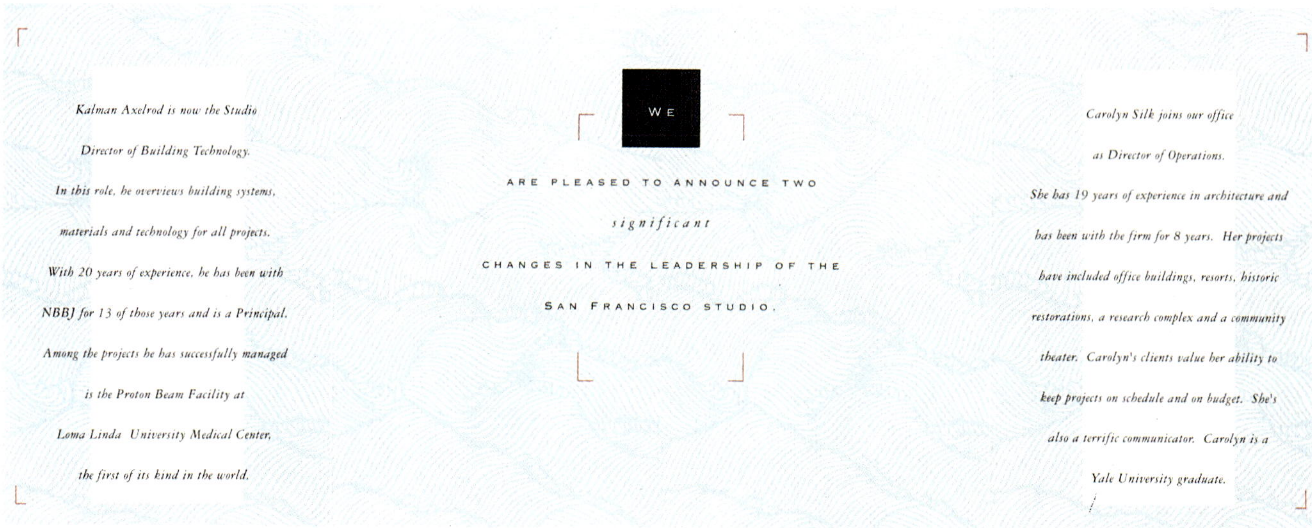

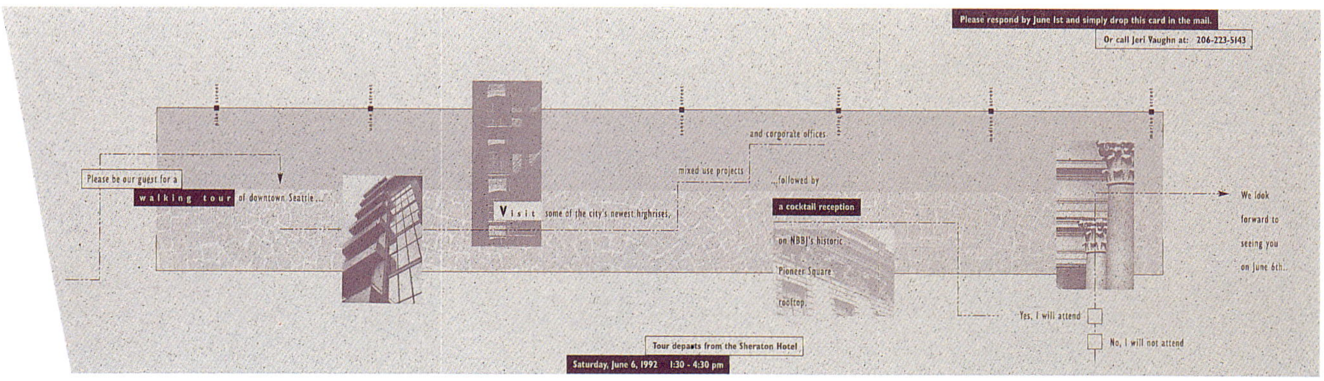

AD: Kerry Burg D: Susan Dewey CW: Steve Heimerle / John Pangrazio DF: NBBJ, Graphic Design Department CL: NBBJ-San Francisco Office USA 1993

AD: Kerry Burg D: Margo Sepanski CW, DF: NBBJ, in-house graphic design group CL: NBBJ USA 1992

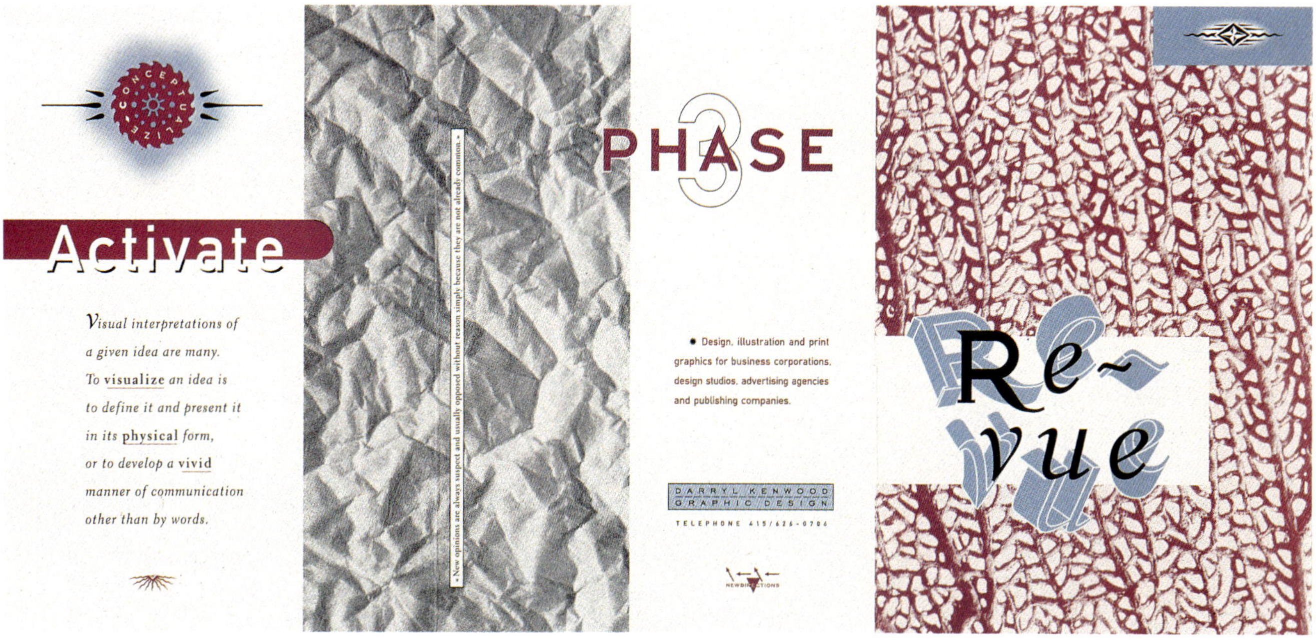

AD: Darryl Kenwood CW: J. E. Garcia / Compose DF: Darryl Kenwood Design CL: Darryl Kenwood Design USA 1993

CD, AD, D, CW: Kristin Sommese CD, AD, I: Lanny Sommese DF: Sommese Design CL: Lanny & Kristin Sommese USA 1991

M

AD, D, CW: Stefanie Choi CL: Don Flynn & Linda Benny USA 1992

AD: Hisao Sugiura D: Toshio Matsuura DF: Studio Super Compass CL: Y's for Men Japan 1991

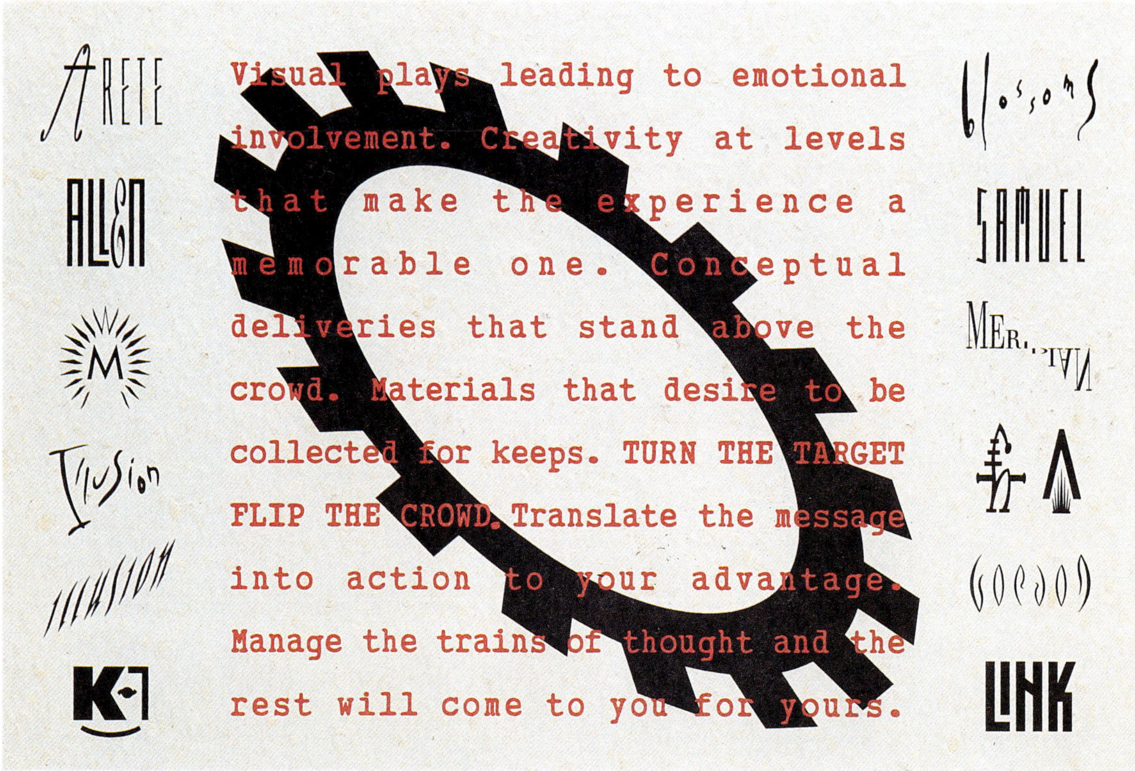

CD, AD, D, I: Carlos Segura DF: Segura CL: Segura USA 1992

AD: Mark Krumel D: Tina Zientarski DF: Rickabaugh Graphics CL: Millcraft Paper USA 1991

CD, AD, D: Keisuke Unosawa DF: Keisuke Unosawa Design CL: Keisuke Unosawa Design Japan 1993

CD, AD, D, I: Anita Meyer Coordinators: Sherri Sommerville / Frank Comella DF: plus design CL: Art Gallery of Ontario USA 1993

D, I: Kurt Dornig DF: Dornig Grafik Design CL: Bertram Strozl Austria 1992

AD: Hisao Sugiura D: Toshio Matsuura / Studio Super Compass DF: Studio Super Compass CL: Y's for Living Japan 1992

F H

F H

CD, AD: Koji Mizutani D: Hiroshi Ohmizo / Junko Horiuchi P: Fumihiko Mizutani I: Hiroshi Ohmizo DF: Mizutani Studio CL: O'Leary Japan 1993

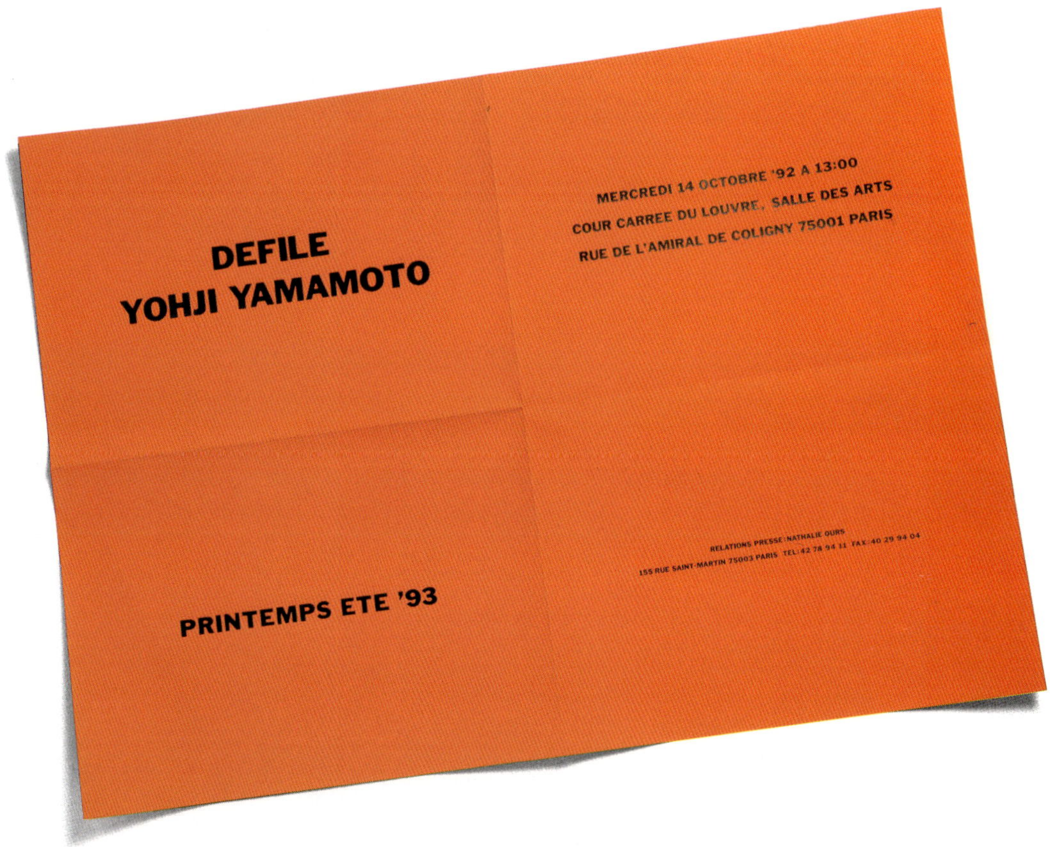

AD: Hisao Sugiura D: Yasunobu Kawajiri DF: Studio Super Compass CL: Y's for Men Japan 1992

AD: Hisao Sugiura D: Yasunobu Kawajiri DF: Studio Super Compass CL: Yohji Yamamoto Japan 1992

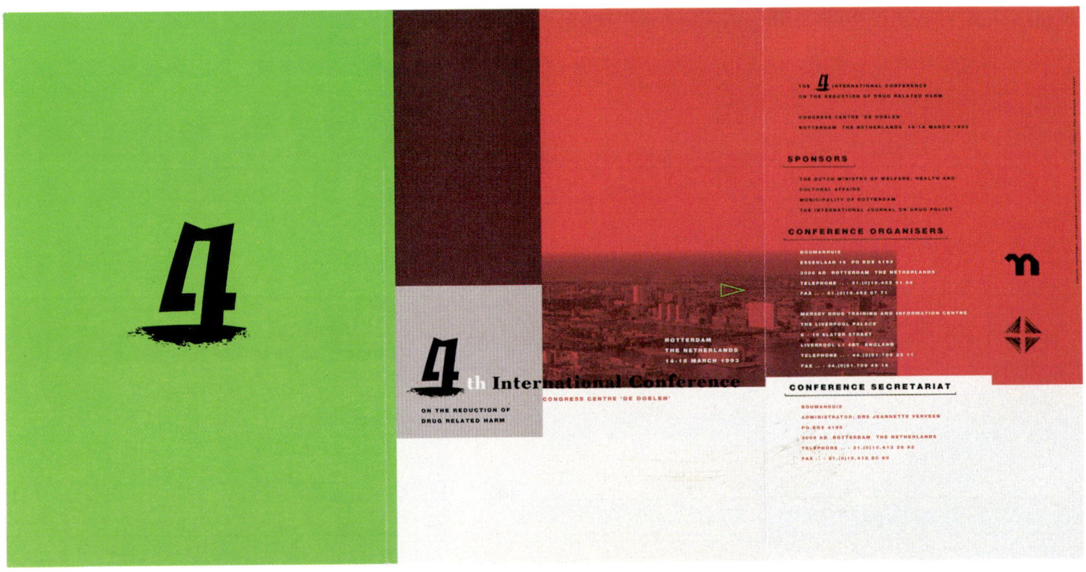

F

D: Michael Snitker DF: Proforma Rotterdam, Association for Design & Consult CL: Boumanhuis Foundation The Netherlands 1993

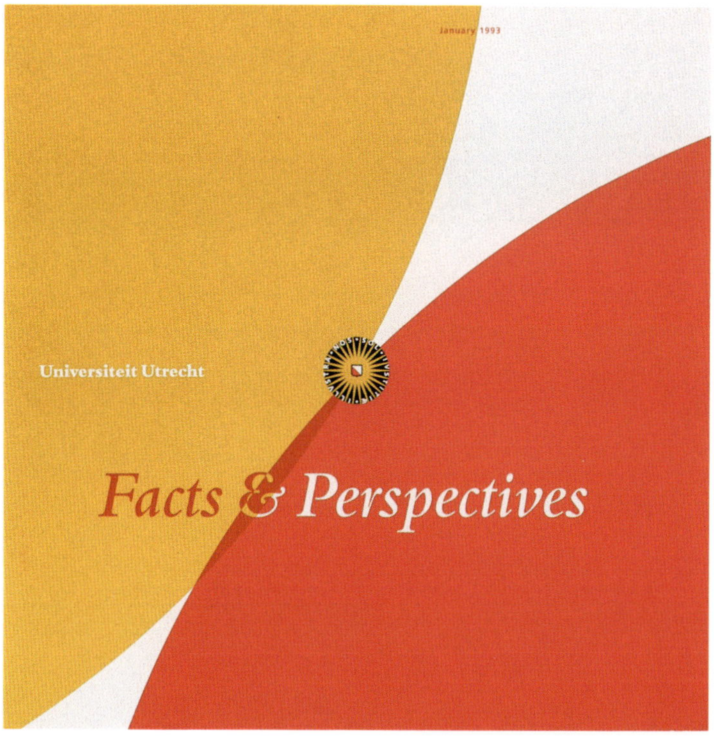

AD, D: Aad van Dommelen D: Ciaran O'Goara / Marc van der Heyde DF: Proforma Rotterdam, Association for Design & Consult
CL: Utrecht University The Netherlands 1992-1993

AD: Raul Cabra D: Rebekah Lee DF: Cabra Diseño CL: San Francisco Art Institute USA 1992-1993

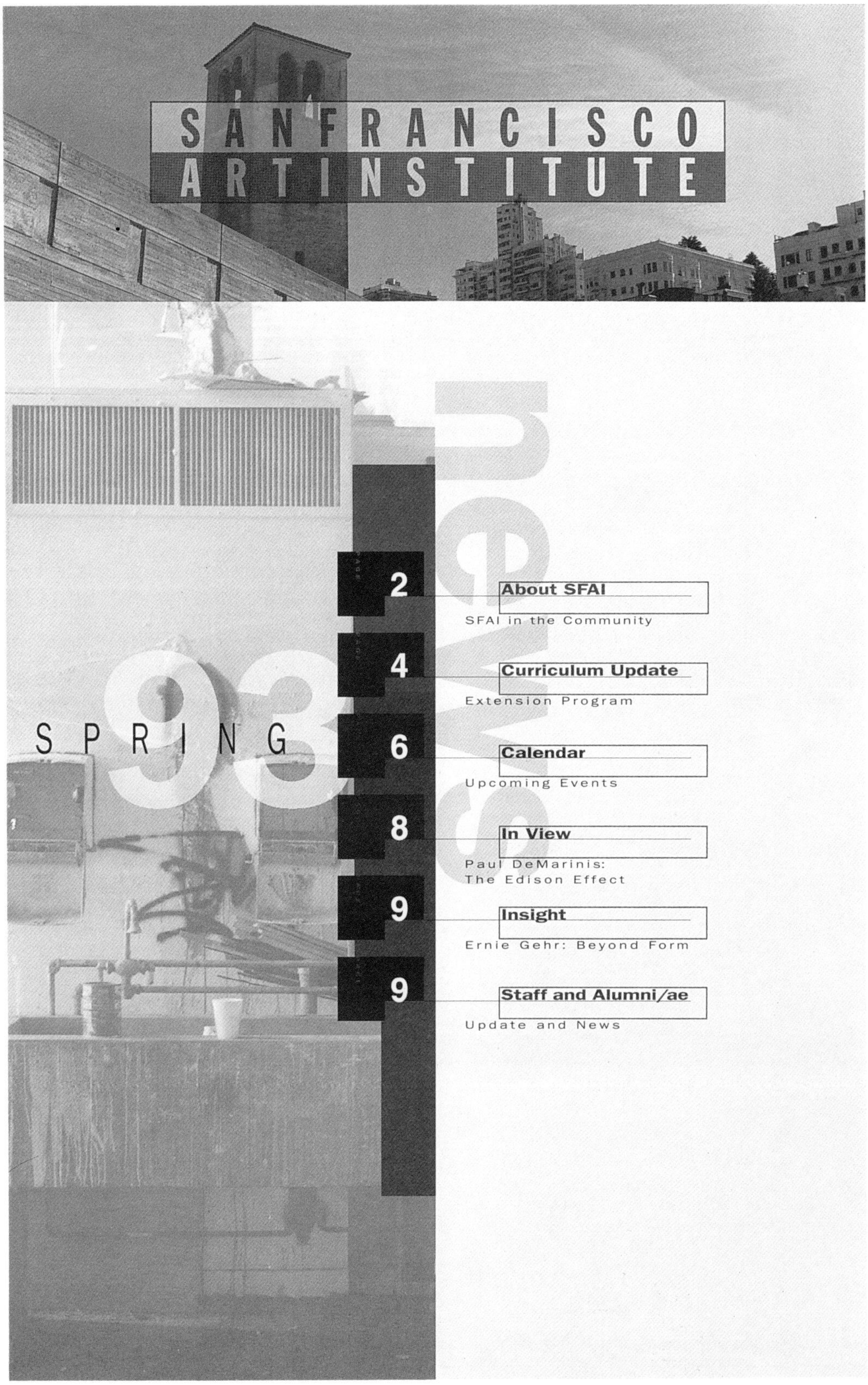

AD: Raul Cabra D: Rebekah Lee DF: Cabra Diseño CL: San Francisco Art Institute USA 1992-1993

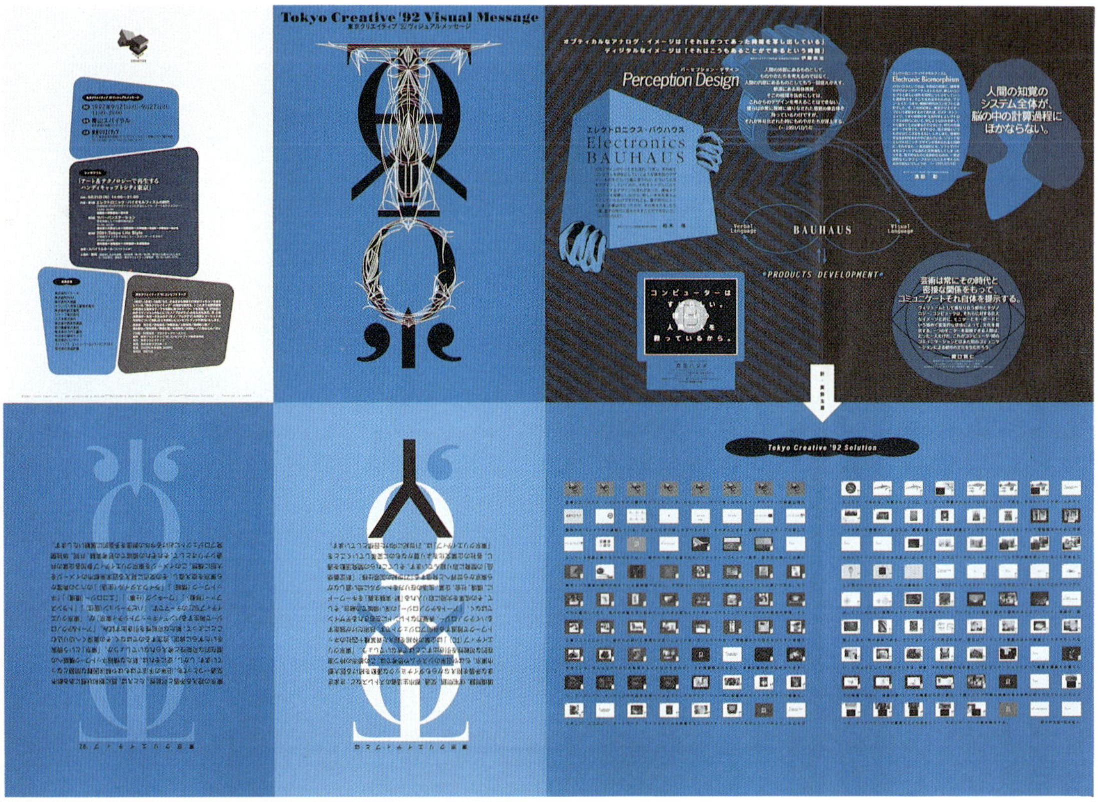

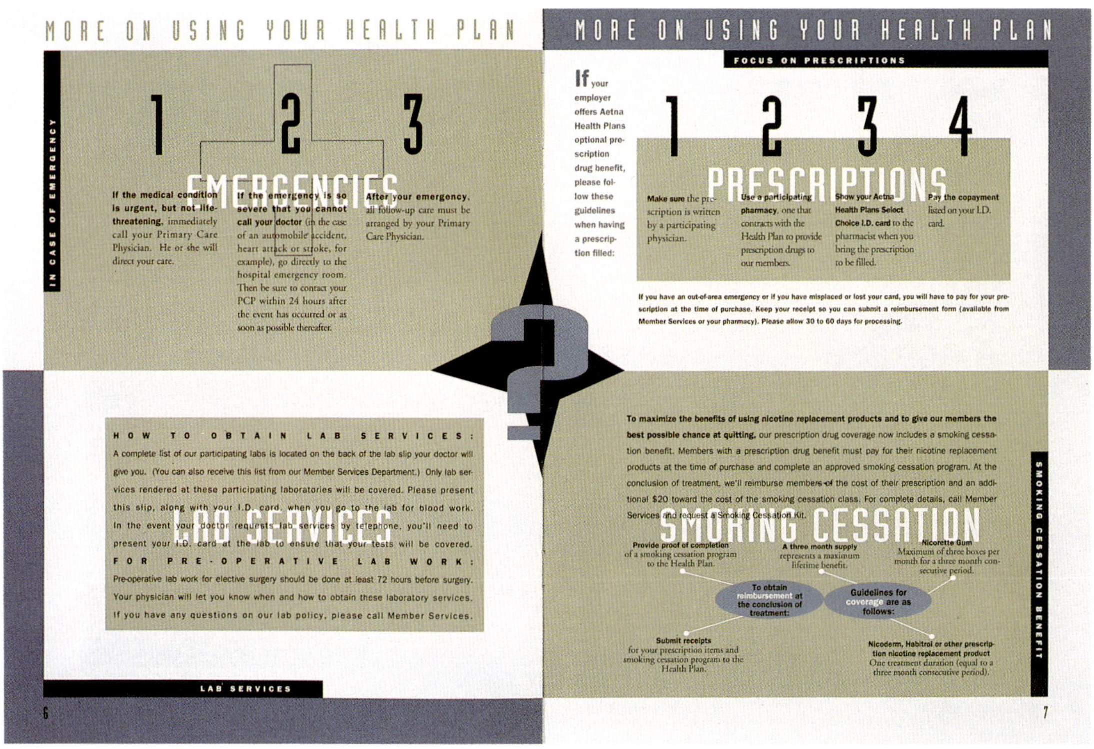

AD: Gento Matsumoto DF: Saru Brunei CL: Tokyo Creative Japan 1992

AD, D: Raul Cabra I: Julia Colmenares DF: Cabra Diseño CL: AETNA Health Plans USA 1993

D: Mirjam van den Haspel DF: Proforma Rotterdam, Association for Design & Consult CL: City of Delft The Netherlands 1992

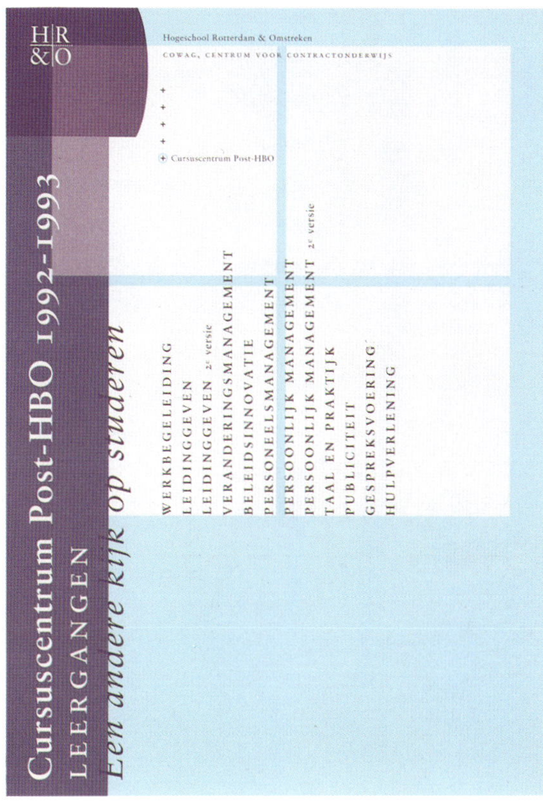

D: Bart de Haas DF: Proforma Rotterdam, Association for Design & Consult CL: Hogeschool Rotterdam, Cowag The Netherlands 1993

CD, AD, D, P: Rudy Vanderlans DF: Emigre CL: Emigre USA 1992

AD: Kerry Burg D: Margo Sepanski / Susan Dewey / Dale Hart / Doug Keyes / Klindt Parker / Stefanie Choi
CW: NBBJ DF: NBBJ (in-house graphic design group) CL: NBBJ USA 1990-1992

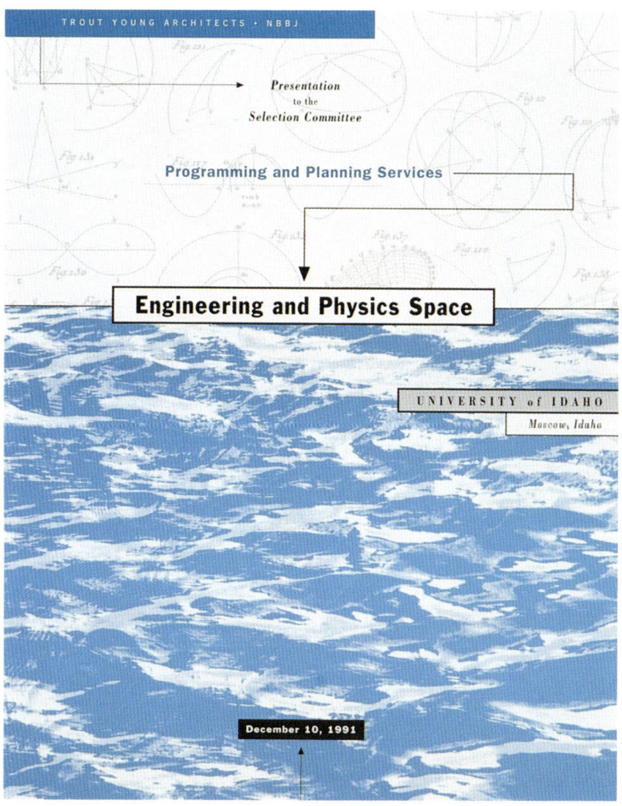

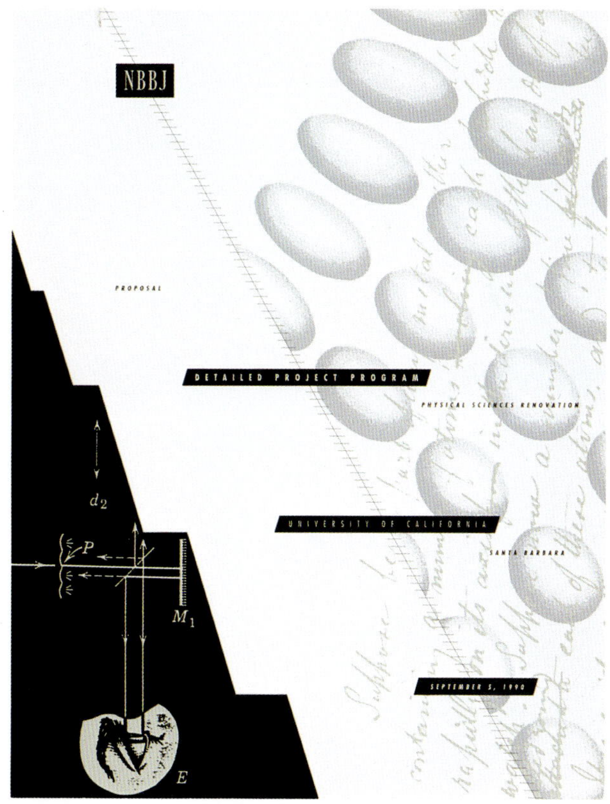

AD: Kerry Burg D: Margo Sepanski / Susan Dewey / Dale Hart / Doug Keyes / Klindt Parker / Stefanie Choi
CW: NBBJ DF: NBBJ (in-house graphic design group) CL: NBBJ USA 1990-1992

AD: Joop Ridder D: Bart de Haas DF: Proforma Rotterdam, Association for Design & Consult CL: TNO Product Centre The Netherlands 1991

D: Michael Snitker DF: Proforma Rotterdam, Association for Design & Consult CL: Recreatie Rotterdam The Netherlands 1993

AD, D: Mrs. M. van den Haspel D: Michael Snitker DF: Proforma Rotterdam, Association for Design & Consult CL: City of Rotterdam The Netherlands 1992

Personalia

pagina 2

Huwelijk | *Marriage*
22/01/93
Dijkwel P., MO-2
Traas A.A.M.
26/02/93
Weeke A.E., MO-3
Bonte B.J.J.
05/03/93
Gabriels L.J.A., 3e Werktuigkundige
Vilters M.J.

Promoties | *Promotions*
Grootenboer W., Hoofdwerktuigkundige
Huybens G.B., 2e Werktuigkundige
Stroosnijder J., Scheepstechnicus

Geslaagd | *Successful examination*
HC Ballieux E.R.
HC Boelens P.F.
HS1 Heugen E.P.R.

De dienst verlaten | *Contract terminated*
Castro J.P., Bediende
Hoogerbrugge M., 3e Werktuigkundige
(Over naar walorganisatie)
Kieboom C.T.J.A. v.d., 3e Werktuigkundige
Linders F.J., Scheepsgezel
Sequeira A., Bediende
Smeeing R., Scheepsgezel
Wicherts H.A., 3e Werktuigkundige

Gedetacheerd | *Secondment*
Alberti M., van Ommeren Shipping
Ent P. van der, North Sea Ferries
Gent W.T.J. van, Afd. LFC
Hoek G.J., Neddrill
Roersma J., Afd. LFC

Tel.nummers

Telefoonbeantwoorder van Nedlloyd Lijnen B.V. te Rotterdam

(010) 4.13.58.14

ms	AMSTELWAL	PCPY
mt	MAASSLOT	PFRS
mt	MAASSTAD	PFRT
mt	MAASSTROOM	PFRU
ms	NL MAAS	PJHA
ms	NL MADRAS	PGDY
ms	NL MAIN	PJIP
ms	NL MANILA	PGDI
ms	NL MARNE	PJHZ
ms	NL MARSEILLES	PGDJ
ms	NL MERWE	PJHB
ms	NL MUSI	PJHL

(010) 4.13.58.25

ms	NL AFRICA	PGCU
ms	NL AMERICA	PGCY
ms	NL ASIA	PGDE
ms	NL CLEMENT	PGDO
ms	NL COLOMBO	PGDL
ms	NL DEJIMA	PGDB
ms	NL DELFT	PGDD
ms	NL EUROPA	PGDF
ms	NL HOORN	PGDC
ms	NL HOUTMAN	PGDR
ms	NL NEERLANDIA	PGEG
ms	NL OCEANIA	PGEA

(010) 4.13.58.66

ms	CASTOR	PDIH
ms	HEEMSKERCK	PJEY
ms	IBN BAJJAH	PGDP
ms	NL VAN DIEMEN	PGFE
ms	NL VAN NECK	PGEB
ms	NL VAN NOORT	PGEC
ms	NL ROCHESTER	PGDZ
ms	NL ROSARIO	PGDX
ms	NL ROTTERDAM	PGEI
ms	NL ROUEN	PGEJ
ms	NL ZEELANDIA	PGDW

Plus artikel

Plus Fleetinfo

Bij de tijd blijven
Om goed op de hoogte te blijven van alle ontwikkelingen die plaatsvinden binnen een bedrijf is het bijzonder belangrijk dat het eigen personeel goed geïnformeerd wordt... In het geval van Nedlloyd Lijnen: wat zijn de doelstellingen van Nedlloyd Lijnen, hoe wil men dit realiseren, wie zit waar... wie vaart waar?
En voor 'wie vaart waar', is Nedlloyd Fleetinfo een hele tijd geleden opgezet. Jaren en jaren is Nedlloyd Fleetinfo volgens dezelfde formule uitgebracht. Het is dus de hoogste tijd dat Nedlloyd Fleetinfo meegaat met zijn tijd. Een nieuw blad met een andere naam: Plus Fleetinfo.

Ander jasje
Wat het eerste opvalt is dat Plus Fleetinfo een ander jasje heeft gekregen. De uitgave is nu opgezet in lijn met het communicatiebeleid van Nedlloyd Lijnen, het zogenaamde Plus-concept. Wij menen dat het blad er voor u nu aantrekkelijker en lezersvriendelijker uitziet.
Bovendien zult u in Plus Fleetinfo (de naam zegt het al) extra (Plus)-info aantreffen. Informatie die nodig is om op de hoogte te blijven van alle belangrijke ontwikkelingen.

Extra info... Plus Fleetinfo
Wat kunt u in de komende uitgaven verwachten?
Plus Who is who
Wie zit waar bij Fleetmanagement... noodzakelijk om gemakkelijk en efficiënt uw collega's bij Fleetmanagement te benaderen.
Plus Nieuwe UCC's
2 nieuwe UCC's zijn in aanbouw. Wat is de stand van zaken. Wat zijn de technische vernuftigheden. Wanneer gaan ze in de vaart.
Plus Waar varen wij
Waarheen varen wij. Welke schepen worden op welke diensten ingezet.
Plus Wist u dat
Overzicht met korte mededelingen, charters in/uit.

In de eerstvolgende uitgave gaan wij dieper in op 'Who is who' bij Fleetmanagement. Veranderingen die hebben plaatsgevonden zijn de overdracht van de afdeling Vlootpersoneel en Labour Relations naar de afdeling Fleetmanagement. Deze afdelingen vielen eerst onder de afdeling Human Resource Management.

Plus... Wij zijn benieuwd of u nog suggesties of concrete bijdragen heeft voor onderwerpen waarover u moet worden geïnformeerd. Als u ideeën heeft wilt u die dan toesturen aan de afdeling Fleetmanagement, de heer W.C. Geistdörfer. Hij is verantwoordelijk voor de inhoud. Mocht u nog leuke foto's, cartoons of andere illustraties hebben die voor publicatie geschikt zijn dan kunt u die toesturen aan de afdeling PR & Sales Promotion, mevrouw Thera Duijndam, coördinator van Plus Fleetinfo.

Wij hopen dat u deze uitgave en alle toekomstige uitgaven met veel plezier zult lezen.

Het Plimsoll merk

Gestoken in rokkostuum en hoge hoed, een kolossale kamera achter zich aan slepend, vormde Samuel Plimsoll een merkwaardig beeld in de Engelse havensteden rond 1870, bij het begin van het windjammer tijdperk. Merkwaardiger nog was de reden die een parlementslid ertoe bracht zich te begeven onder de zeelui, waarvan de meeste geen enkel bezit en dus ook geen stemrecht hadden.
Met een aan fanatisme grenzend elan nam Plimsoll in 1870 een kruistocht op zich tegen wat hij 'drijvende doodkisten' noemde; onveilige vrachtschepen, zowel zeil- als stoomschepen, waar ieder jaar honderden zeelieden de dood mee vonden. Geconfronteerd met sterke oppositie in het Parlement, ging Plimsoll de zwaarste misbruiken vastleggen en publiekelijk aanhang werven. Het resultaat in 1873 was 'Our Seamen'; een boek dat met schokkende praktijkvoorbeelden en officiële statistieken aantoonde dat te zware belading en onzeewaardige conditie van de schepen de voornaamste oorzaken waren van vele Engelse scheepsrampen. Plimsoll illustreerde zijn boek met droevige verhalen -zoals over een betraande zeemansweduwe die zich met moeite in leven houdt met naaiwerk bij het licht van een zolderraampje- en met foto's van bleke weduwen met grimmige gezichten, omringd door een zwerm in zwarte klederdracht gestoken vaderloze kindertjes.

Het boek, dat de schuld van de vele ongelukken bij vrekkige reders en een onverschillige overheid legde, sorteerde het gewenste effect. In 1875 werd in het Lagerhuis een wet voorgedragen met één van Plimsoll's belangrijkste maatregelen; een merk op de zijde van de schepen om de maximale diepgang aan te geven. Maar in hetzelfde jaar stelde premier Disraeli voor om de maatregel te herroepen, waarschijnlijk onder druk van afladers die stelden dat de wet buitenlandse concurrenten zou bevoordelen. Plimsoll sprong overeind en beschuldigde de reders in het Parlement van moorddadige praktijken door de wet uit te stellen. Terwijl Plimsoll uit het Parlement naar buiten stormde, liet zijn vrouw vanaf de publieke tribune vlugschriften met een samenvatting van Plimsoll's protest op de lager gelegen perstribune fladderen.
De uitbarsting van Plimsoll haalde de voorpagina's en dwong het Parlement uiteindelijk de 'Unseaworthy Ships Bill' aan te nemen. De wetgever liet de uitvoering echter over aan de reders en sommige van hen schilderden het merk spottend op het bovendek van hun schepen. Pas in 1890 machtigde het Parlement het Ministerie van Handel om het *Plimsoll* op een vast plaats aan te brengen.
Tegen 1930 hadden de meeste landen deze maatregel overgenomen.

Plus fleetinfo

Tweemaandelijkse uitgave van Nedlloyd Lijnen B.V. Postbus 240 3000 DH Rotterdam **14e jaargang nr. 1, februari 1993**

Monsterrol — pagina 1
Personalia — pagina 2
Tel.nummers — pagina 2
Plus artikel | *Introductie Plus Fleetinfo* | *Het Plimsoll merk* — pagina 2

Plus fleetinfo
Nedlloyd Lijnen B.V. Postbus 240 3000 DH Rotterdam

Nedlloyd Lines

Port betaald - Port Payé
Rotterdam - Pays Bas

AD: Mirjam van den Haspel D: Michael Snitker DF: Proforma Rotterdam, Association for Design & Consult CL: Nedlloyd Lines The Netherlands 1993

D: Ian Swift CL: Polystar Japan 1993

D: Mirjam van den Hospel DF: Proforma Rotterdam, Association for Design & Consult CL: Technical University Eindhoven The Netherlands 1992

CD, AD, D, I: John Sayles CW: Adam Katzman DF: Sayles Graphic Design CL: Western Regional Greek Conference USA 1993

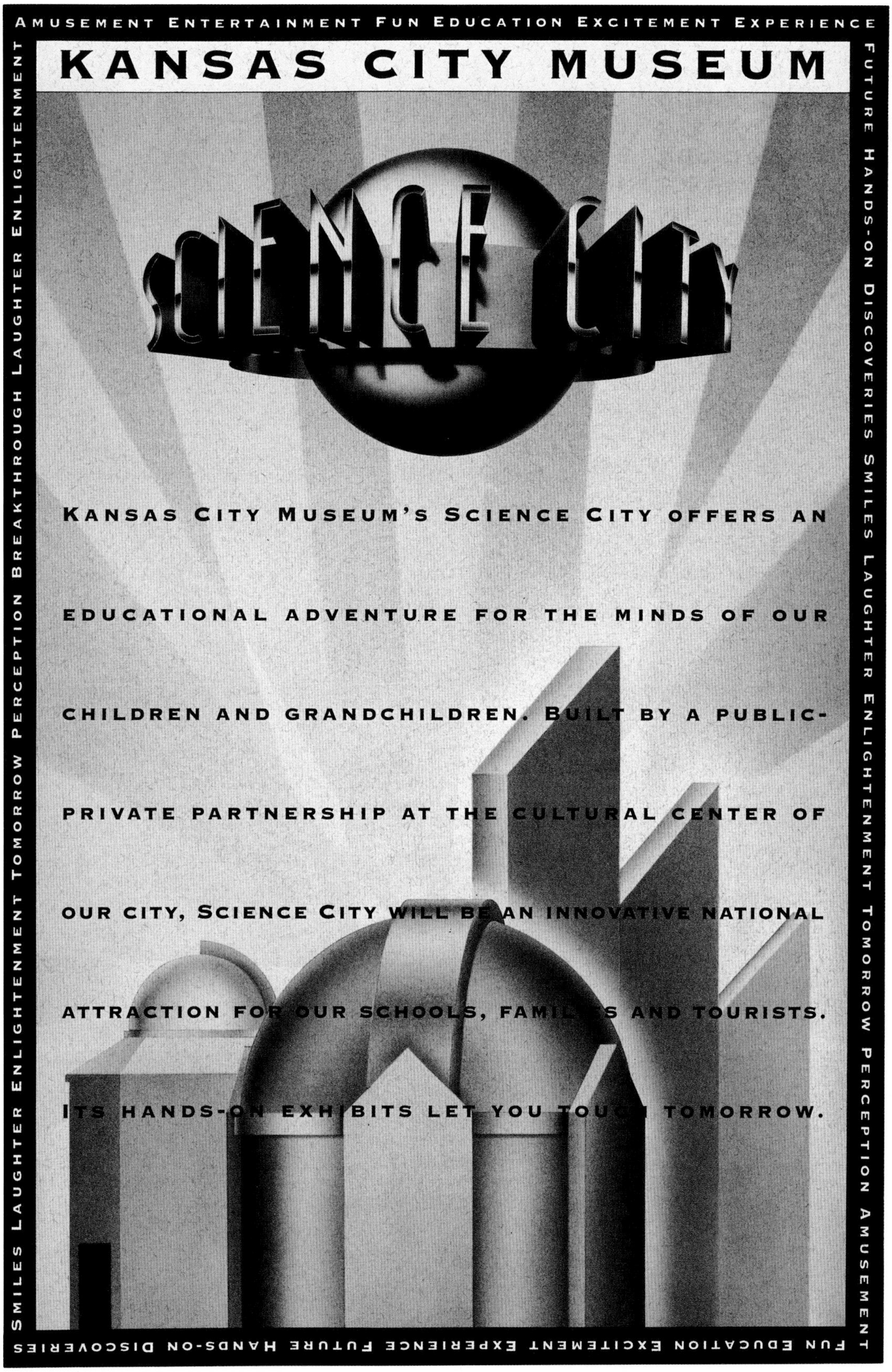

AD, D: John Muller D: Scott Chapman I: Marty Roper CW: Doug Edwards DF: Muller + Company CL: Kansas City Museum USA 1992

D, P: Brian Smith CL: Brian Smith USA 1993

CD, AD, D: Carlos Segura DF: Segura / Gandelman Advertising CL: The Merchandise Mart USA 1992

D: Aad van Dommelen DF: Proforma Rotterdam, Association for Design & Consult CL: City of Rotterdam The Netherlands 1991

T

AD, D, I: J. Graham Hanson DF: J. Graham Hanson Graphic Design CL: Mr. & Mrs. Frank S. Owens USA 1992

AD: Kerry Burg D: Stefanie Choi CW: NBBJ DF: NBBJ (in-house graphic design group) CL: NBBJ USA 1992

AD: Paul Browning D, I: Peter Baker DF: Taylor & Browning Design Associates CL: KPMG Peat Marwick Thorne Canada 1989

D: Mirjam van den Haspel DF: Proforma Rotterdam, Association for Design & Consult CL: Rotterdamse Kunststichting The Netherlands 1990

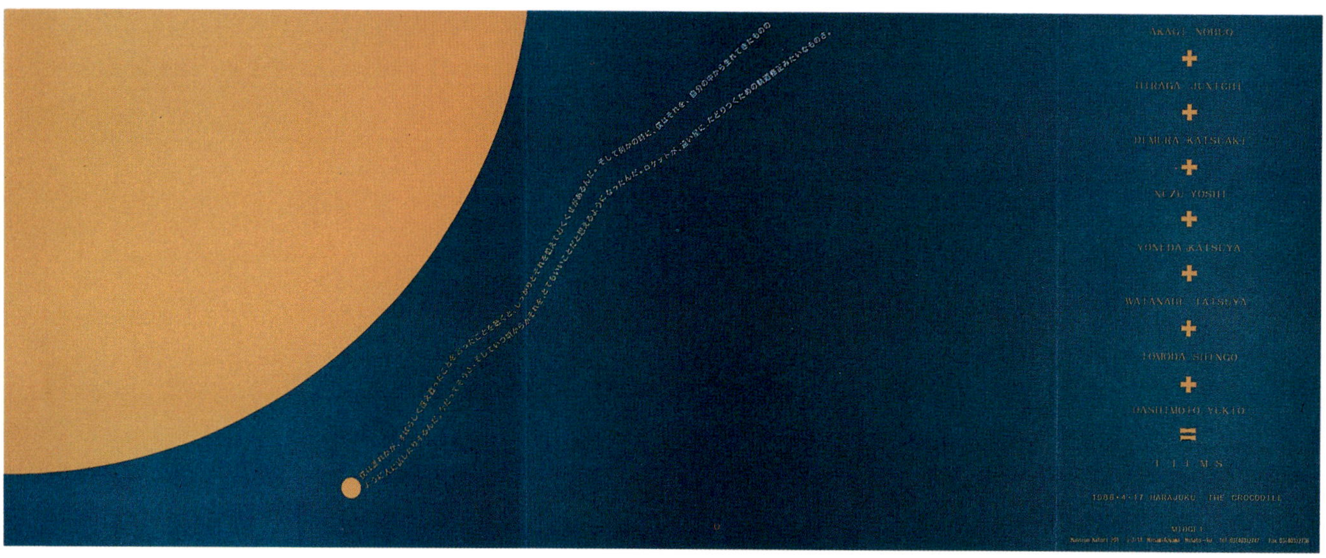

CD, AD, D, I: Keisuke Unosawa DF: Keisuke Unosawa Design CL: Midget Japan 1988

CD, AD, D, I: Keisuke Unosawa DF: Keisuke Unosawa Design CL: Midget Japan 1988

CD, AD, D, I: Keisuke Unosawa DF: Keisuke Unosawa Design CL: Midget Japan 1988

CD, AD, D, I: Keisuke Unosawa DF: Keisuke Unosawa Design CL: Midget Japan 1988

IWACO
Adviesbureau voor water en milieu
Jaarverslag 1992

IWACO

12

Onderzoek monitoring- en beheersmaatregelen van de Coupépolder, Alphen aan den Rijn

Voor de provincie Zuid-Holland heeft IWACO een onderzoek verricht naar de monitoring- en beheersmaatregelen met betrekking tot de vuilstort in de Coupépolder. De beheersmaatregelen hebben zich gericht op het wegnemen van de directe risico's voor volksgezondheid en milieu. Directe risico's bestonden er door percolaatuittreding langs de taluds en naar het omringende oppervlaktewater. Zij-afdichtingen bestaande uit kleilagen en een ringdrainagesysteem zijn hiervoor ontworpen en reeds aangebracht.

Omdat het diepe grondwater onder en ten noorden van de stort verontreinigd zal raken, ontstaan er op langere termijn risico's voor de volksgezondheid. Om deze te kunnen bepalen moest behalve een monitoringsysteem een geohydrologisch beheerssysteem worden ontworpen. Het monitoringsysteem is ontworpen met behulp van MODISCO. Deze methode, die werkt op basis van een door IWACO ontwikkeld GIS-systeem, maakt het mogelijk monitoringsystemen met een gekwantificeerde trefkans te ontwerpen.
In de vorm van een saneringsonderzoek is, met behulp van een geohydrologisch model, de meest gunstige variant bepaald voor het geohydrologisch beheerssysteem.
Gekozen is voor een variant bestaande uit een zevental putten die zich ten noorden van de stort bevinden. Met behulp van een beslismodel worden de meetresultaten van het monitoringsysteem vertaald naar eventueel te nemen beheersmaatregelen.
In het beslismodel zijn de technische en organisatorische aspecten vastgelegd van de nazorg van de Coupépolder.

Vooruitzichten Jaarverslag 1992

13

Ondanks de stagnerende economische groei in Noordwest-Europa zien wij de toekomst met optimisme tegemoet. De sectoren milieu en economie hebben immers veel gemeen: in beide gevallen gaat het om het zorgvuldig omspringen met schaarse middelen.
IWACO speelt daarop in door professionaliteit te koppelen aan creativiteit bij het uitvoeren van opdrachten voor de overheid en het particuliere bedrijfsleven.

Wij verwachten dat onze activiteiten in Nederland de komende jaren in bescheiden mate zullen toenemen, zeker als we deze afzetten tegen de forse groei van de afgelopen jaren. Onze inspanningen zullen vooral gericht zijn op verdere professionalisering en verbreding van onze dienstverlening op het gebied van water, bodem, afvalstoffen en (industrieel) milieu in ruimere zin. De rode draad die door onze inspanningen heen komt te lopen, zal bestaan uit het aandragen van creatieve, pragmatische oplossingen, gefundeerd op een gezonde basis van deskundigheid ten aanzien van alle aspecten die meespelen in ons milieu.

Wij verwachten de komende jaren een relatief sterke toename van onze activiteiten in België en Duitsland. Het succes van de eerste structurele stappen, die wij in onze buurlanden in 1992 hebben gezet, geven alle aanleiding voor deze positieve prognose. Wij beschouwen deze stappen tevens als essentieel voor het proces van verdere internationalisering van onze Europese dienstverlening gedurende de rest van de jaren negentig. In het verlengde van de UNCED milieuconferentie verwachten wij hernieuwde internationale aandacht voor de water- en milieuproblematiek in Azië en Afrika.
De in Nederland beschikbare kennis en ervaring op het gebied van beleidsontwikkeling, planvorming en technologie staat internationaal hoog aangeschreven. Wij voorzien dan ook een groeiende markt voor adviesdiensten op dit terrein.

D: Mirjam van den Haspel P: Joachim Jager DF: Proforma Rotterdam, Association for Design & Consult
CL: Iwaco, Consultancy on Water & Environment The Netherlands 1993

CD, AD, D, DF: Koeweiden / Postma P: YANi CL: YANi, Amsterdam The Netherlands 1992

CD, AD: Richard Bonner-Morgan CD, AD, D: Kate Tregoning D: Robert Taylor DF: Nice CL: Film & Video Umbrella England 1990

CD, AD: Richard Bonner-Morgan CD, AD, D: Kate Tregoning DF: Nice CL: Film & Video Umbrella England 1991

CD, AD: Richard Bonner-Morgan CD, AD, D: Kate Tregoning DF: Nice CL: Film & Video Umbrella England 1992

CD, AD: Richard Bonner-Morgan CD, AD, D: Kate Tregoning DF: Nice CL: Film & Video Umbrella England 1993

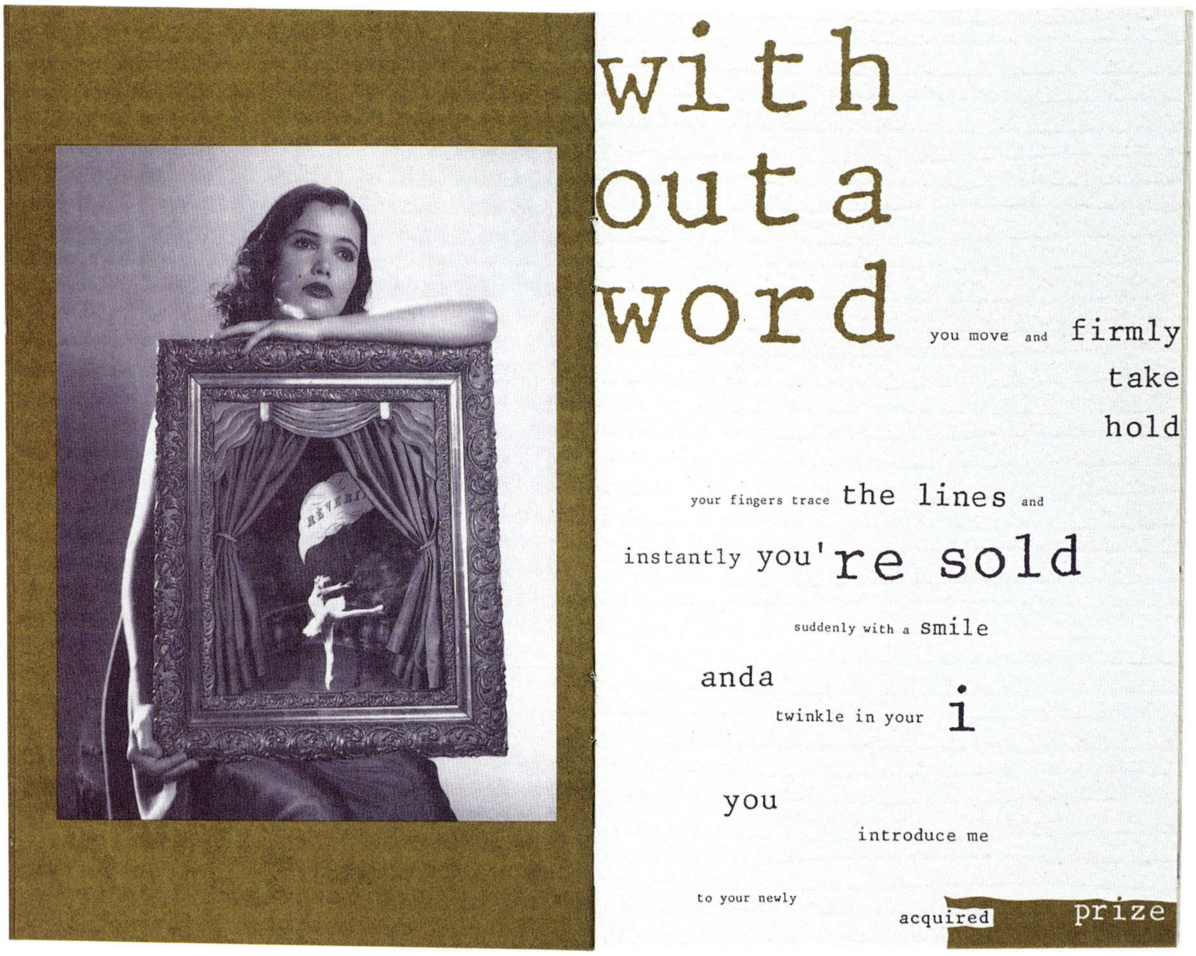

AD, D: Jeff Fabian / Jean Kane / Sam Shelton P: Geof Kern CW: Cheryl Duvall CL: Design Industries Foundation for AIDS, DC Chapter USA 1991

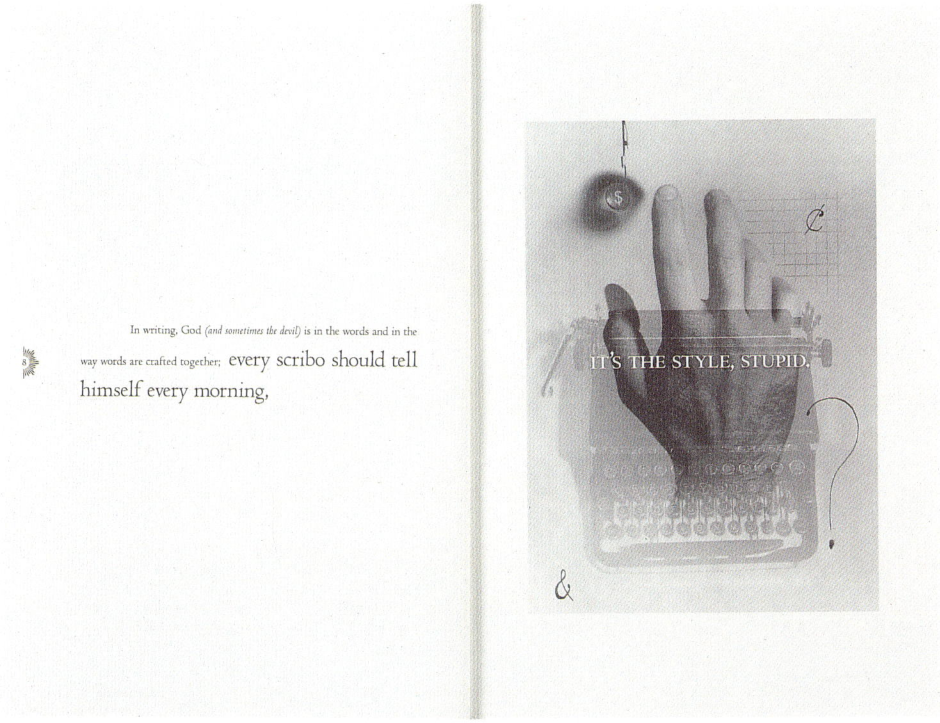

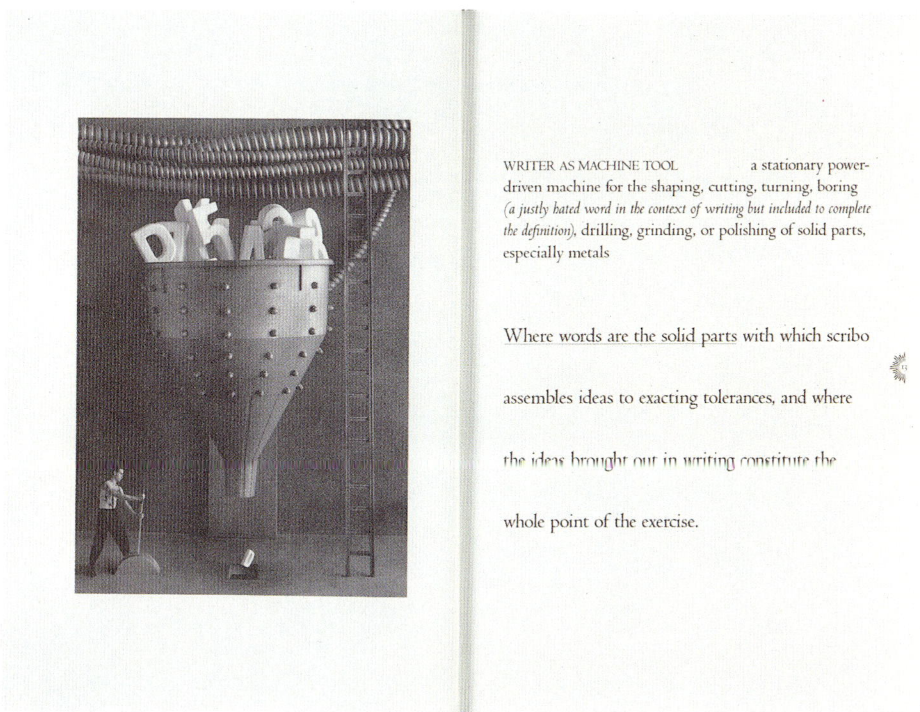

CD, AD, D: Carlos Segura P: Geof Kern DF: Segura CL: John Cleland USA 1993

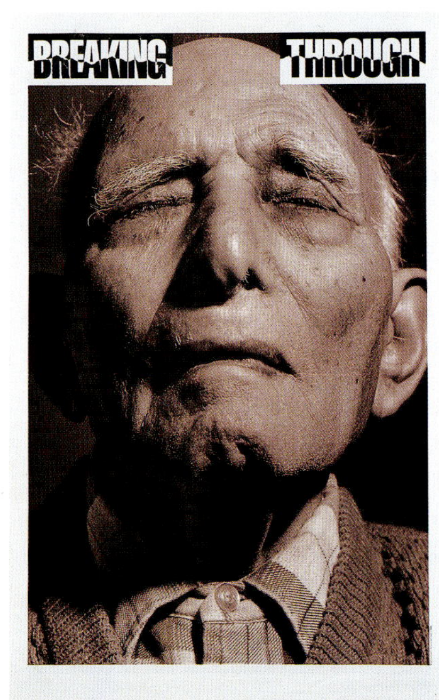

AD, D: John Muller / Patrice Eilts / Lee Ernst / Jane Weeks / Kent Mulkey D, CW: David Marks
P: Hollis Officer / Nick Vedros DF: Muller + Co. CL: The Art Directors Club of Kansas City USA 1989

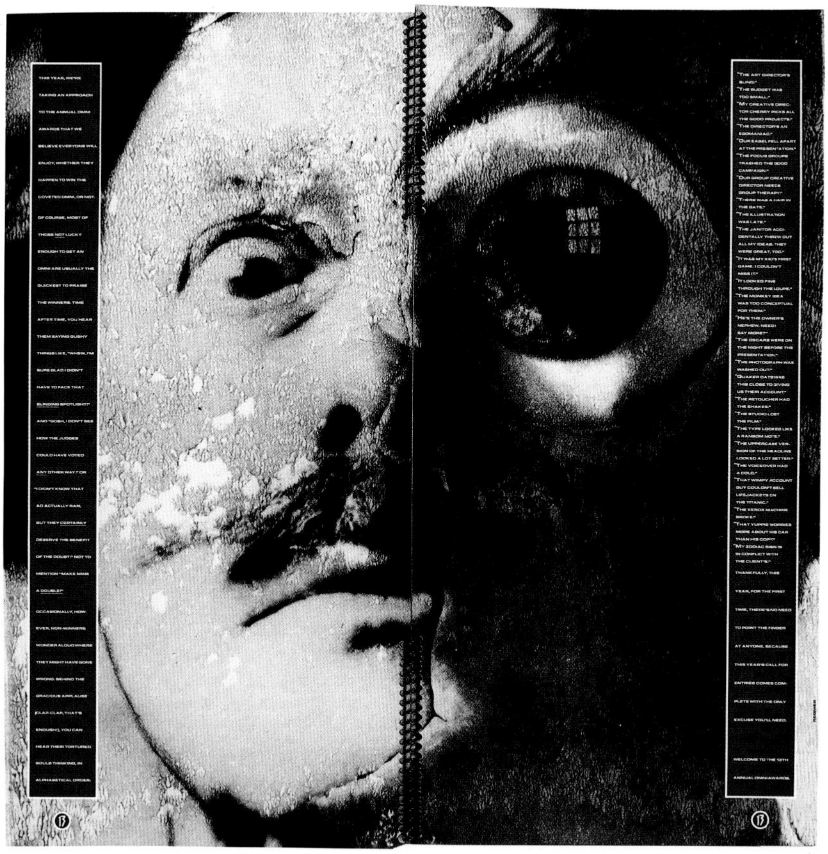

AD: John Muller D: Jane Weeks CW: David Marks DF: Muller + Co. CL: KC AD Club USA 1991

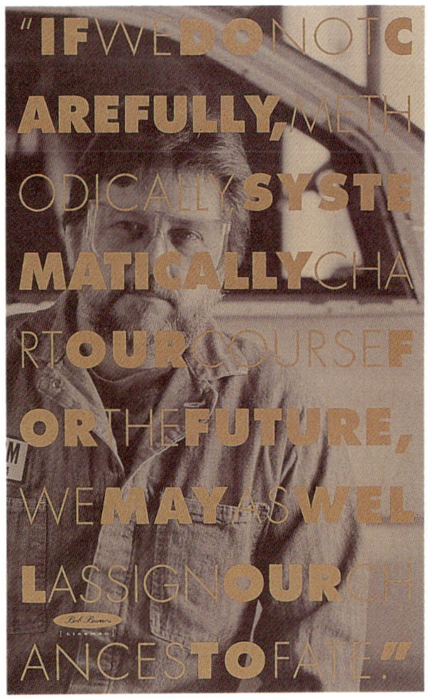

G

AD: John Muller D: Susan Wilson / David Shultz P: Dan White DF: Muller + Co. CL: Kansas City IABC USA 1993

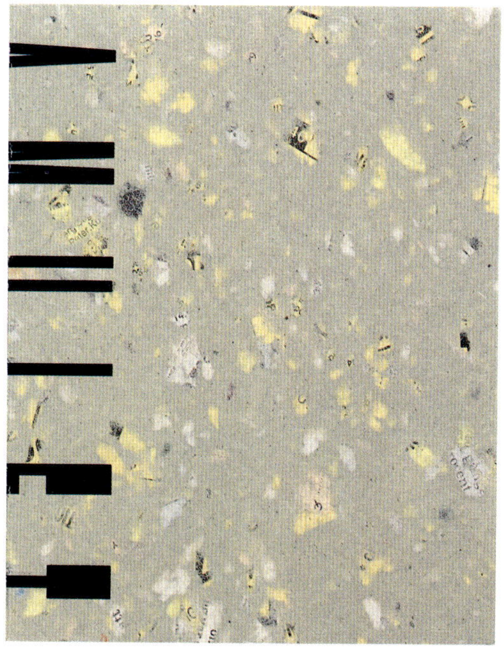

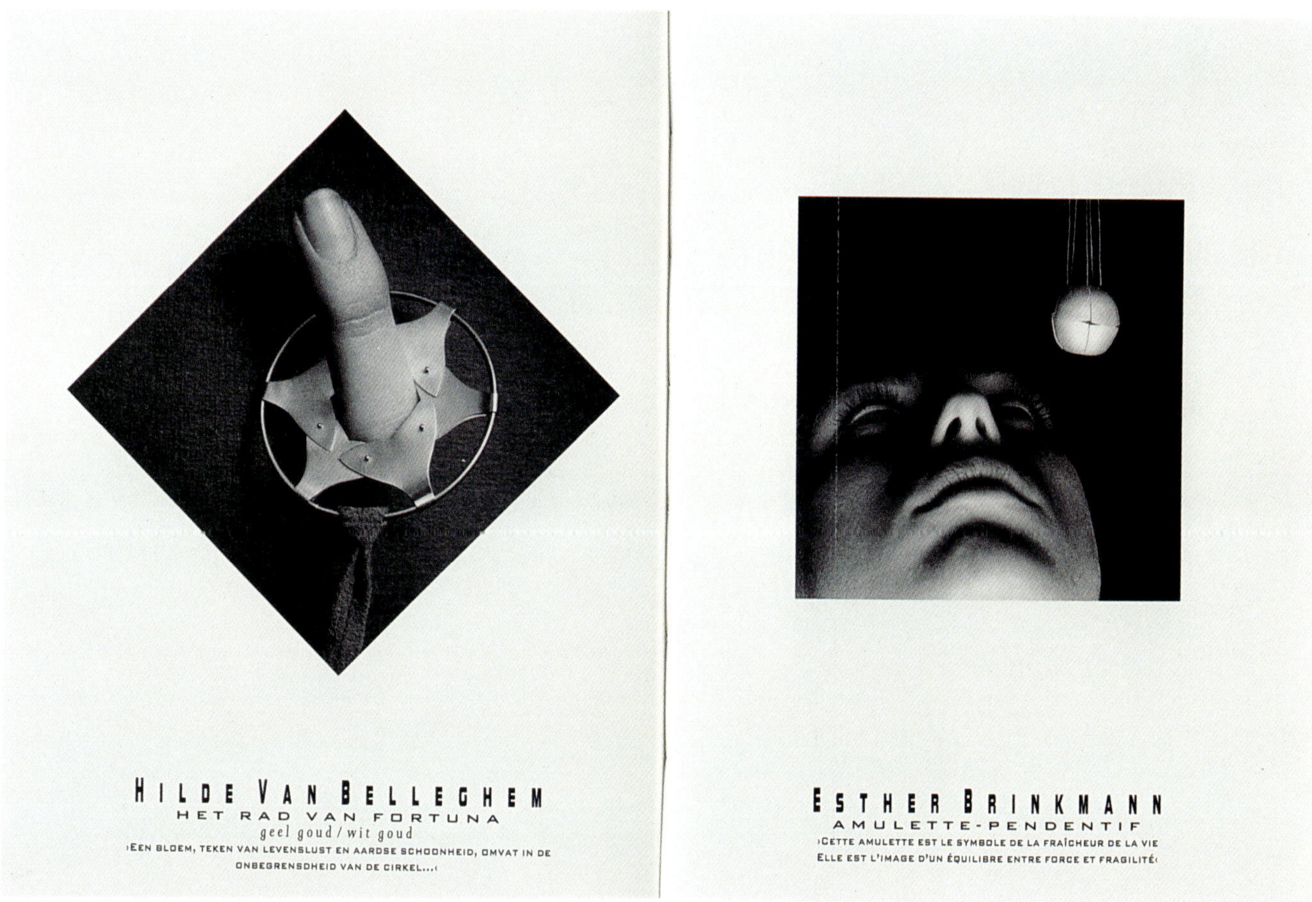

D: Henrik Barends DF: Studio Henrik Barends CL: Gallery Marzee The Netherlands 1993

AD: John Muller P: Mike Regnier CW: David Marks DF: Muller + Co. CL: Muller + Co. USA 1992

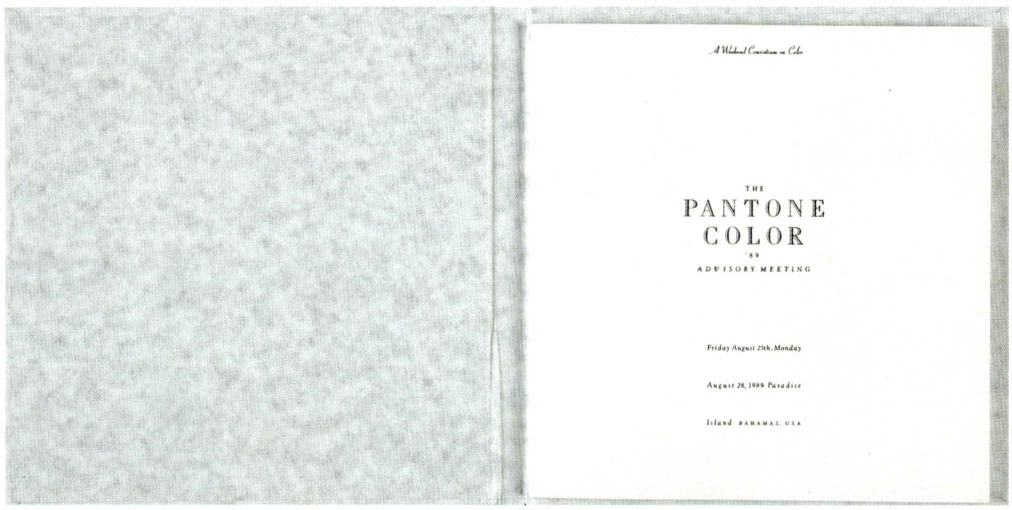

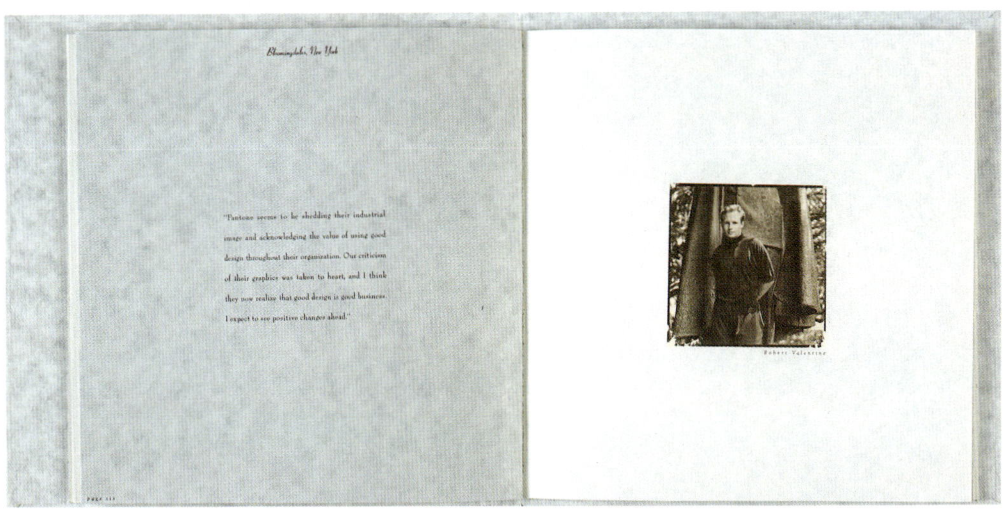

CD, AD, D: Charles S. Anderson D: Daniel Olson P: James Williams CW: Lisa Pemrick DF: Charles S. Anderson Design CL: Pantone USA 1990

CD, AD: Richard Seireeni D: Romane Cameron P: Phillip Dixon DF: Studio Seireeni CL: Jun USA 1992

CD: Robert Bergman-Ungar P: Matthew Rolston CL: Bloomingdale's USA 1988

C

Brand: Hiroko Koshino CD, AD: Koji Mizutani D: Hiroshi Ohmizo P: Katsuo Hanzawa DF: Mizutani Studio CL: Hiroko Koshino Design Office Japan 1991

CD, AD, P: Katsu Asano D: Kinue Yonezawa / Nobuko Yamamoto P: Taka Kobayashi DF: ASA 100 Company CL: Barreaux Division Scoop Japan 1992

CD, AD, P, I: Katsu Asano D: Kinue Yonezawa DF: ASA 100 Company CL: Lunetta BADA Japan 1989

G S

AD: Paul Marciano D: Samantha Osselaer P: Ellen Von Unwerth CW: Emily Corey DF: Guess? (in-house) CL: Guess? USA 1991

AD: Paul Marciano D: Samantha Gibson P: Ellen Von Unwerth CW: Emily Corey DF: Guess? (in-house) CL: Guess? USA 1991

M M

CD, AD, P, I: Katsu Asano D: Kinue Yonezawa / Nobuko Yamamoto P: Taka Kobayashi DF: ASA 100 Company CL: Barreaux Division Scoop Japan 1992

CD, AD: Rolf Hunsinger D, I: Thomas Elsner P: Ellen von Unwerth DF: MPS Presse Service CL: Strehle GmbH & Co KG (Streness-Group) Germany 1992

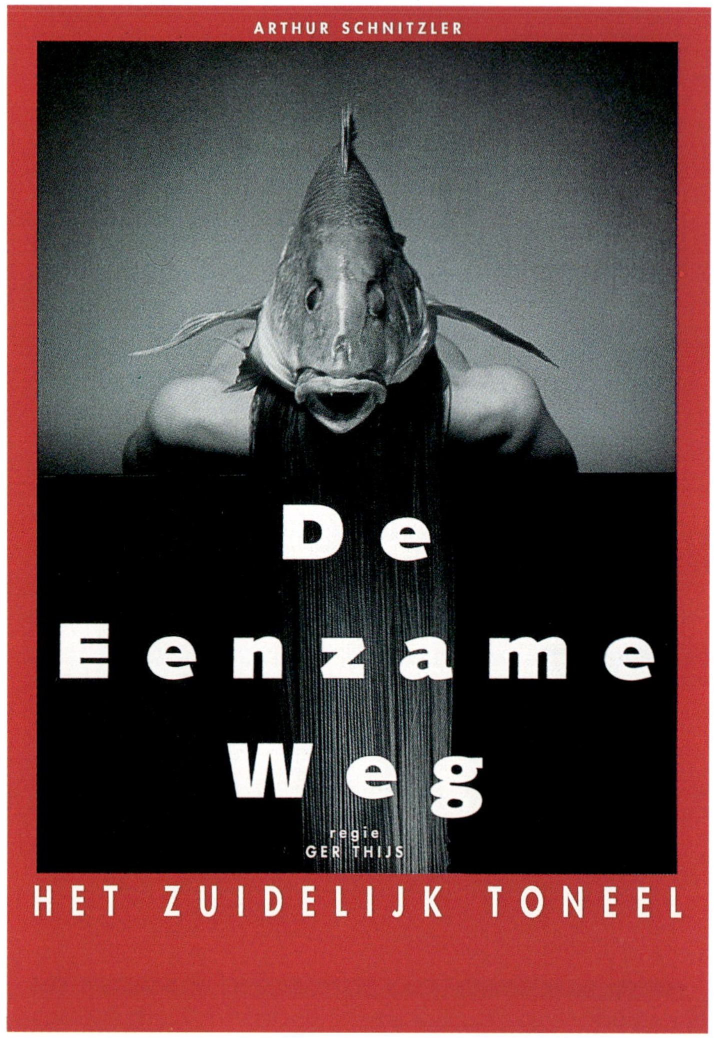

D: Kees Wagenaars P: Erwin Olaf DF: Opera Grafisch Ontwerpers CL: Het Zuidelijk Toneel The Netherlands 1992

D: Kees Wagenaars P: Erwin Olaf DF: Opera Grafisch Ontwerpers CL: Het Zuidelijk Toneel The Netherlands 1992

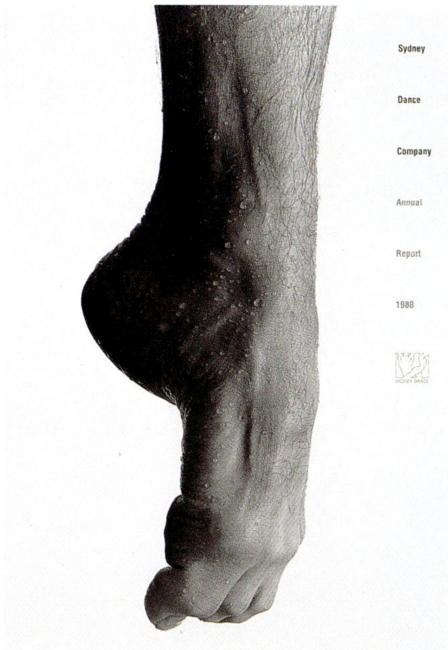

CD, AD, D: Phil Ritchie P: Mark Ritchie DF: Ritchie Thorburn Design CL: Sydney Dance Australia 1989

AD: Ichiro Mitani D: Yoko Nakamura P: Gakuji Tanaka DF: Mitani Ichiro Design Studio CL: A Gathering of 6 Ceramists Japan 1993

林克次

6

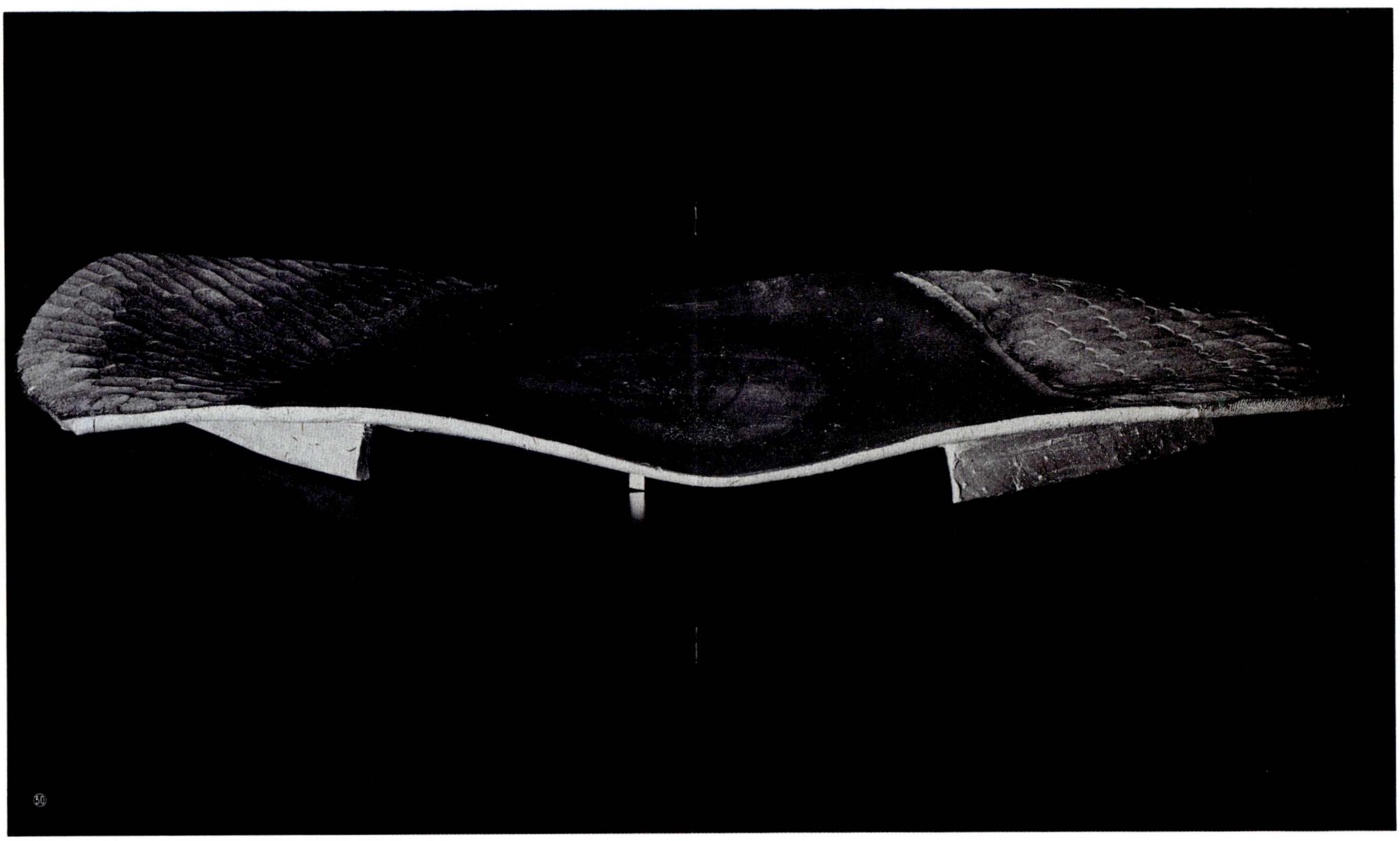

AD, D: Ichiro Mitani P: Gakuji Tanaka DF: Mitani Ichiro Design Studio CL: Dept. of Fine Arts Division Takashimaya Japan 1991

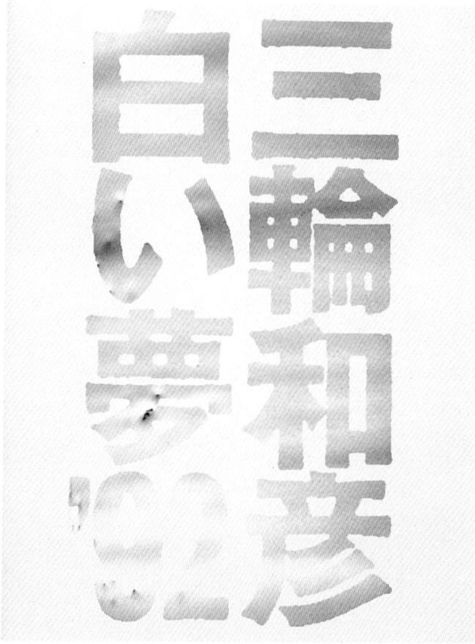

AD: Ichiro Mitani D: Yosuke Hasegawa P: Gakuji Tanaka DF: Mitani Ichiro Design Studio CL: Kazuhiko Miwa Japan 1992

號外!
決定版「唐十郎＝作 金盾進＝演出」今秋スズナリにてロングラン決定!
少女都市からの呼び声
2つの「少女都市からの呼び声」にご期待ください!
2ヴァージョン決定!
Aヴァージョン(10/28—11/14)
田口……黒沼弘巳
雪子……石井ひとみ
フランケ醜態博士……金守珍
有沢……近藤弐吉
ビンコ……洲永敬子
他梁山泊一同出演
◆音楽……小室等
Bヴァージョン(11/16—11/23)
田口……六平直政
雪子……金久美子
フランケ醜態博士……金守珍
有沢……近藤弐吉
ビンコ……洲永敬子
他梁山泊一同出演
◆音楽……安保由夫
スタッフ
舞台監督……村松明彦＋ZEST
舞台美術……小竹信節
照明デザイン……沖野隆一
照明オペレーター……ステージング
音響効果……EASTONE
振付……大川妙子
制作……新宿梁山泊事務所
日時＝1993年10月28日(木)—11月23日(火)※15日休演
夜7時開演(土日マチネ2時あり・祭日マチネ2時のみ)
場所＝下北沢ザ・スズナリ
料金＝前売・電話予約2800円/当日3000円
お問い合わせ＝新宿梁山泊事務所 03-3380-5827
HARUMIドーム21受付(3/6—3/14)にて、特別先行予約受付中!(一般前売開始8月予定)
会場にて直接ご予約の方先着50名様に「少女都市からの呼び声」
スズナリ版特製ポスター引換券を差し上げます
コラージュ……小竹信節 号外作成……佐藤直樹
◎やる気のある新人随時募集中!
(詳細は事務所宛お電話下さい。3380-5827)
新宿梁山泊

AD, D: Koji Ise CL: Studio Zoo Japan 1990

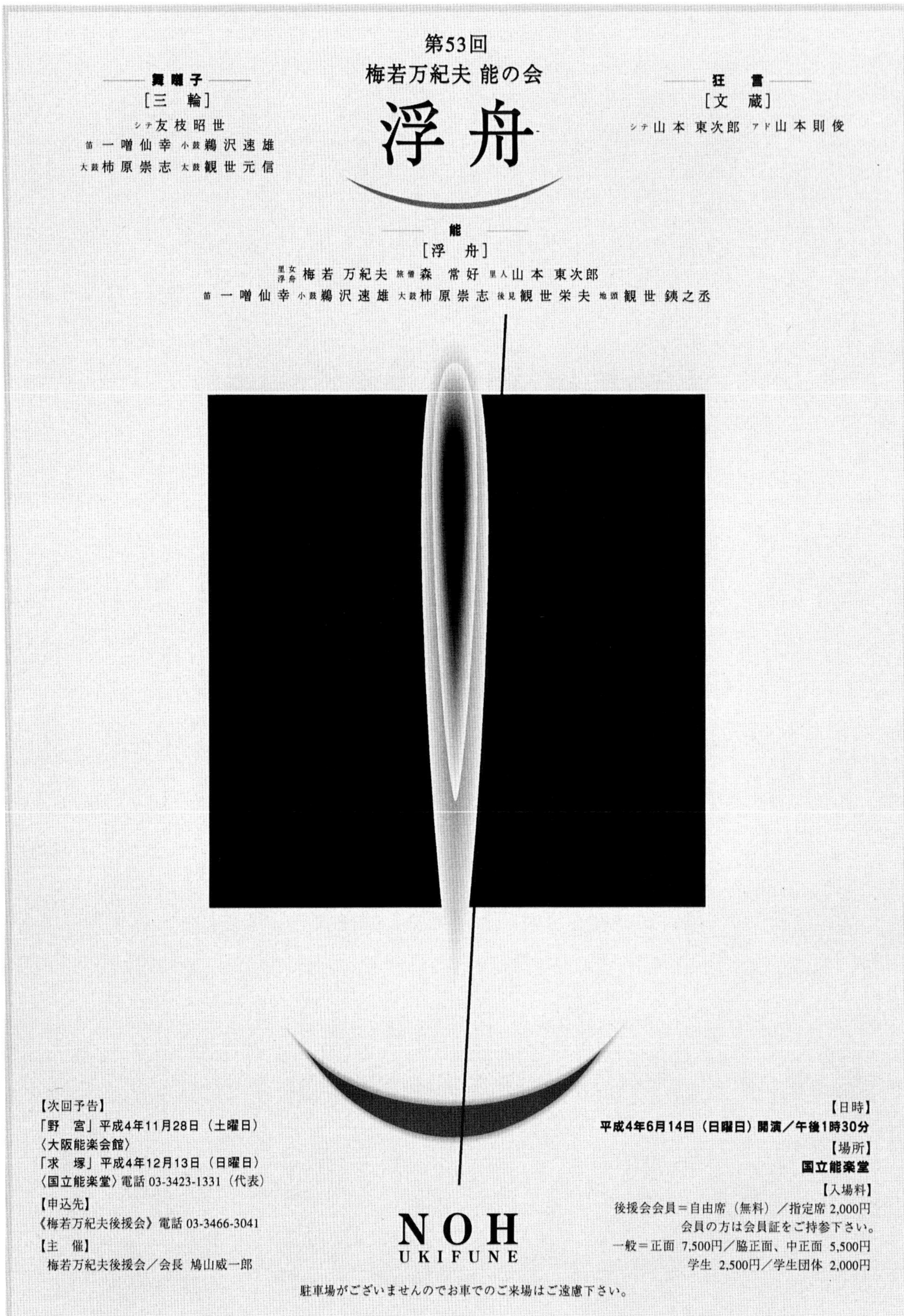

AD, D: Mutsuo Yamauchi CL: A Society for the Support of Makio Umewaka Japan 1992

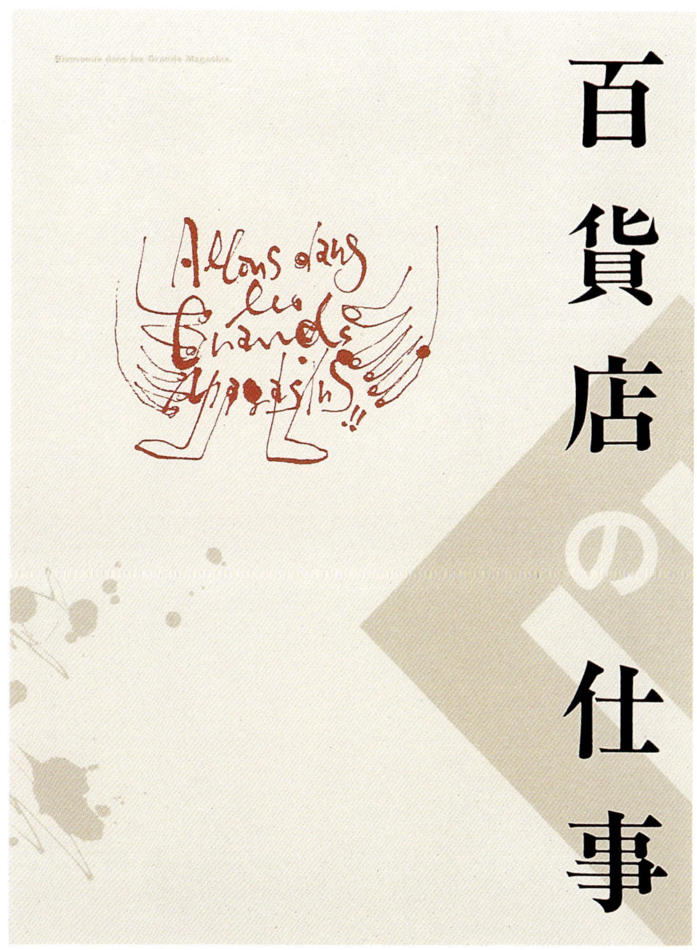

CD, AD: Kan Tai-keung AD, D: Eddy Yu Chi Kong D: Joyce Ho Ngai Sing P: Franklin Lau
DF: Kan Tai-keung Design & Associates CL: The Community Chest of Hong Kong Hong Kong 1991

CD: Yasuo Kyobe AD, D: Naoki Sato I: Masami Nozue DF: Tetsuzo CL: Japan Department Stores Association Japan 1992

CD, AD, I: Lanny Sommese D: Mark Smith DF: Sommese Design CL: Central Pennsylvania Festival of the Arts USA 1992

CD, AD, I: Lanny Sommese D: Jack Simmen DF: Sommese Design CL: Central Pennsylvania Festival of the Arts USA 1990

AD: Eric Rickabaugh D, I: Mark Kruwel I: Tony Meuser CW: Charles Fenton DF: Rickabaugh Graphics CL: Ohio Arts Council USA 1992

D, I: Tom Schifanella DF: Robin Shepherd Studios CL: Tom Schifanella USA 1992

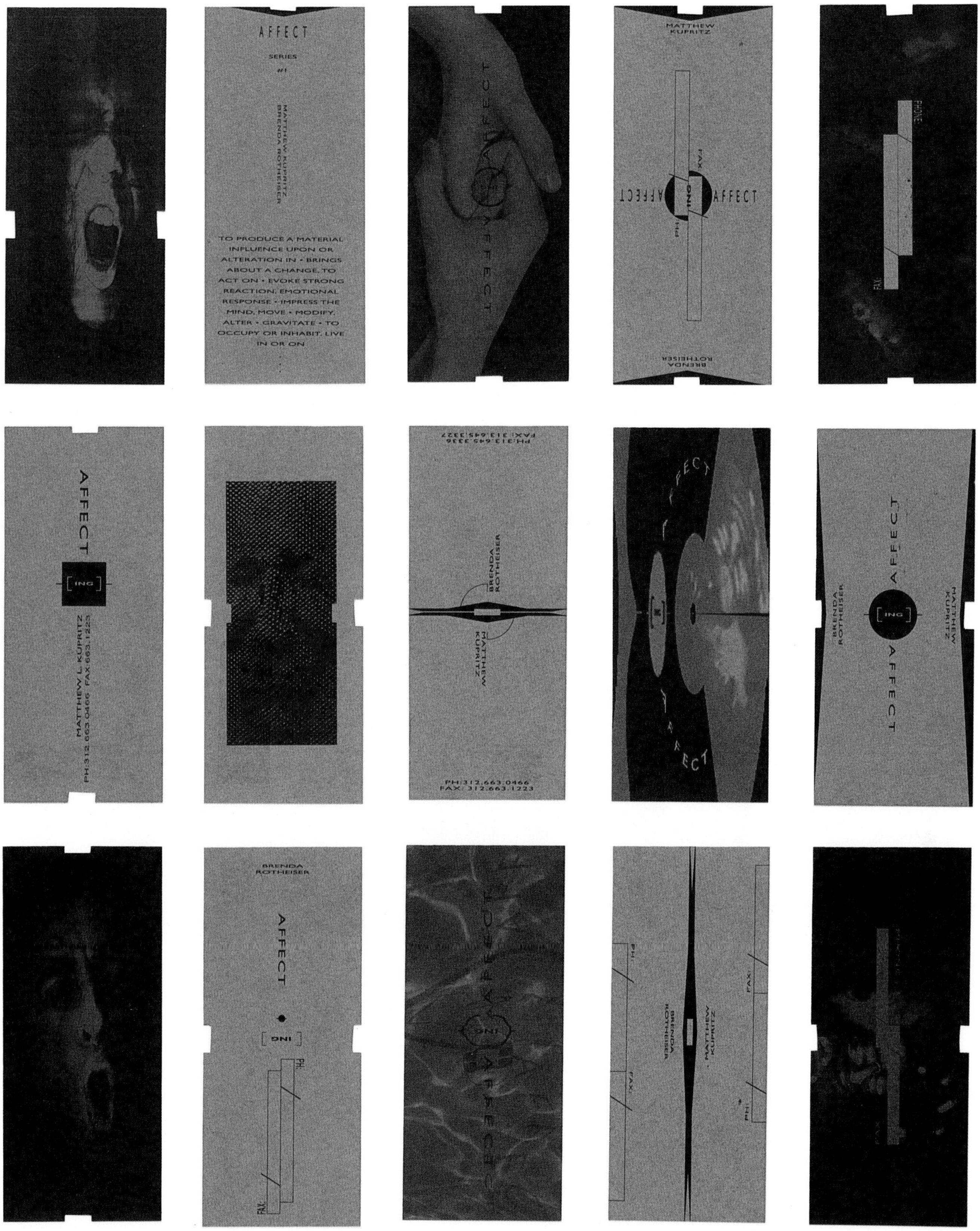

D: Brenda Rotheiser DF: Cranbrook Academy of Art, Department of Design CL: Affect ing USA 1992

D: Henrik Barends DF: Studio Henrik Barends CL: Paul de Nooijer The Netherlands 1989

D: Henrik Barends DF: Studio Henrik Barends CL: Leo Versteijlen The Netherlands 1990

AD, D: Yoshiro Kajitani DF: Kajitani Design Room CL: Cover Japan 1993

CD, AD, D: Doug Gordon I: Steve Myers CL: Cafe Tropical USA 1992

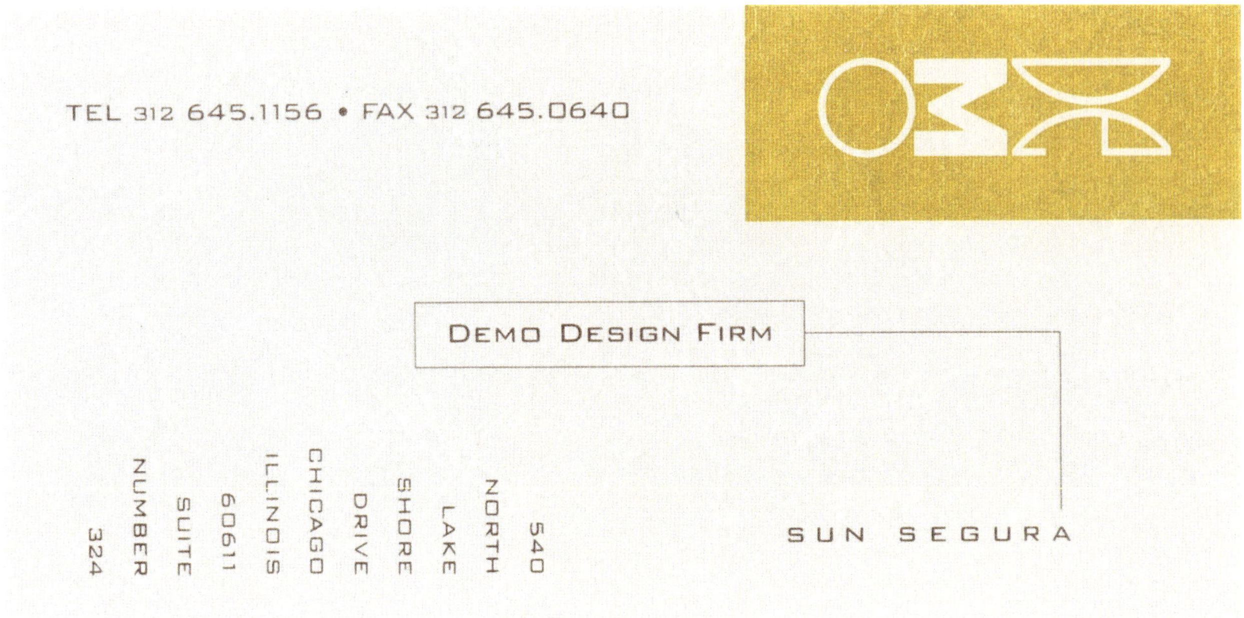

CD, AD, D: Carlos Segura DF: Segura CL: Demo Design USA 1991

AD, D: J. Graham Hanson P: Jeremy Clifford DF: J. Graham Hanson Graphic Design CL: Baby Face Children's Playwear USA 1992

CD, AD, I: Katsu Asano D: Kinue Yonezawa P: Taka Kobayashi DF: ASA 100 Company CL: Barreaux Division Scoop Japan 1993

CD, AD: Katsu Asano D: Kinue Yonezawa P: Kazuhiro Kobayashi DF: ASA 100 Company CL: Barreaux Division Scoop Japan 1992

CD: Andy Ewan AD: Nicola Penny D: Lynne Joddrell P: Daniel Allan CW: Maddy Morton DF: The Yellow Pencil CL: Arts Council England 1992

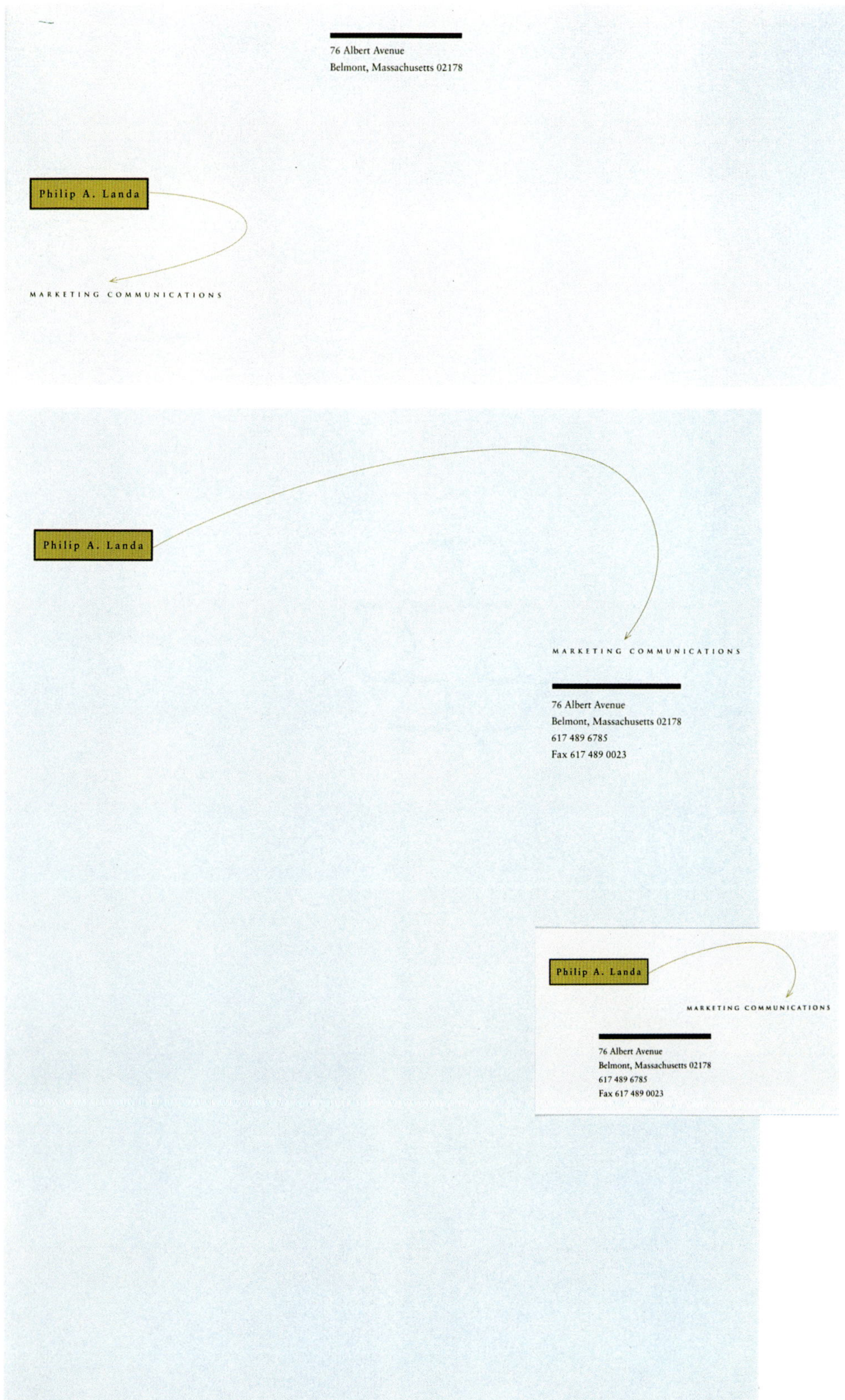

AD: Kathy Forsythe D: Jane Cuthbertson DF: Forsythe Design CL: Phil Landa USA 1993

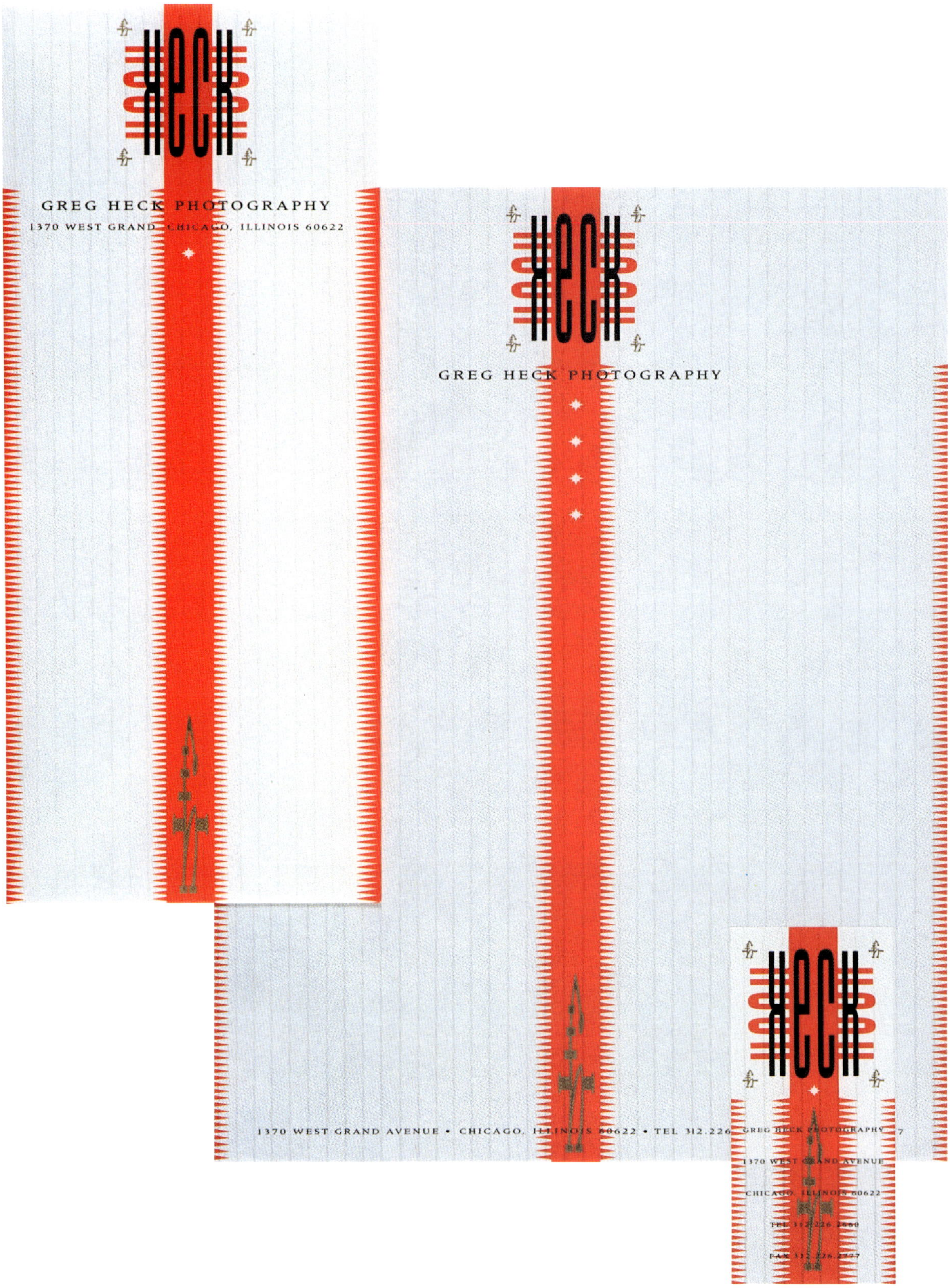

CD, AD, D, I: Carlos Segura DF: Segura CL: Greg Heck Photography USA 1992

AD, D: Mrs. Mirjam van den Haspel D: Michael Snitker DF: Proforma Rotterdam, Association for Design & Consult CL: City of Rotterdam The Netherlands 1992

CD, AD, D, I: John Sayles CW: Wendy Lyons DF: Sayles Graphic Design CL: Adventure Lighting USA 1992

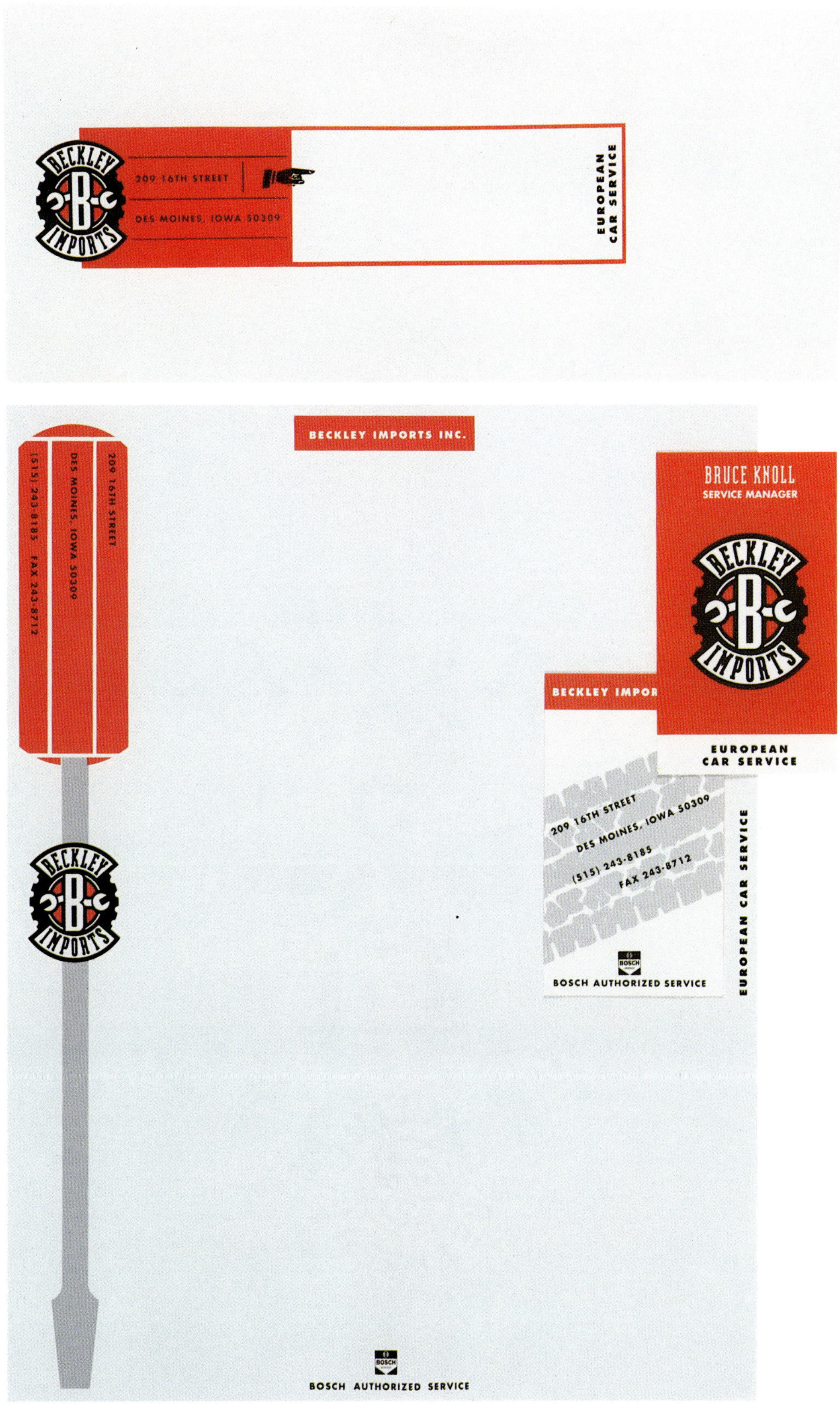

CD, AD, D, I: John Sayles DF: Sayles Graphic Design CL: Beckley Imports USA 1993

CD, AD, D: Carlos Segura P: Geof Kern DF: Segura CL: The Merchandise Mart USA 1992

CD, AD, D: Clifford Stoltze DF: Clifford Stoltze Design CL: Stoltze Design USA 1993

M M

AD: Mark Timmings D: Mario Godbout DF: Turquoise Design CL: Galerie Jean-Claude Bergeron Canada 1992

D: Mirjam van den Haspel DF: Proforma Rotterdam, Association for Design & Consult CL: Bernie Brilman PCO The Netherlands 1991

H
AD, D, I: Mitsunobu Murakami DF: Graphic Laboratory CL: Kadokawa Shoten Publishing Japan 1993

H
AD, D: Masaaki Hiromura D: Takafumi Kusagaya DF: Hiromura Design Office CL: Bungeisyunjyu Japan 1993

D, I: Naoki Sato Publisher: Akifumi Doi CL: Tom's Box Japan 1990

D: Susumu Tada I: Hitoshi Sawano CL: Sangokan Japan 1993

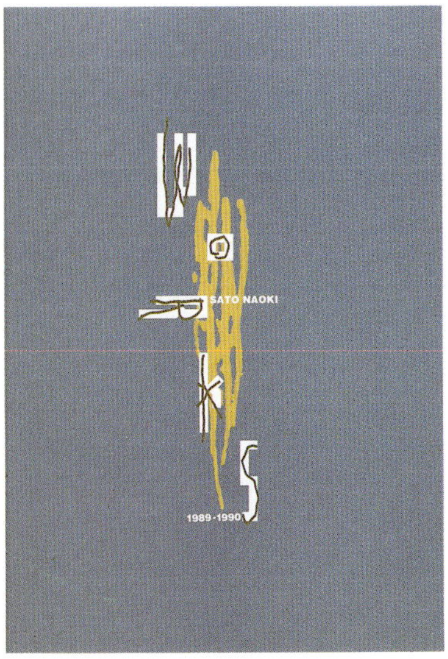

D, I: Naoki Sato Publisher: Akifumi Doi CL: Tom's Box Japan 1990

D: Fred Bower CL: Fred Bower USA 1993

AD, D, P: Mitsuo Shindo DF: Contemporary Production CL: Seibundo Shinkosha Publishing Japan 1993

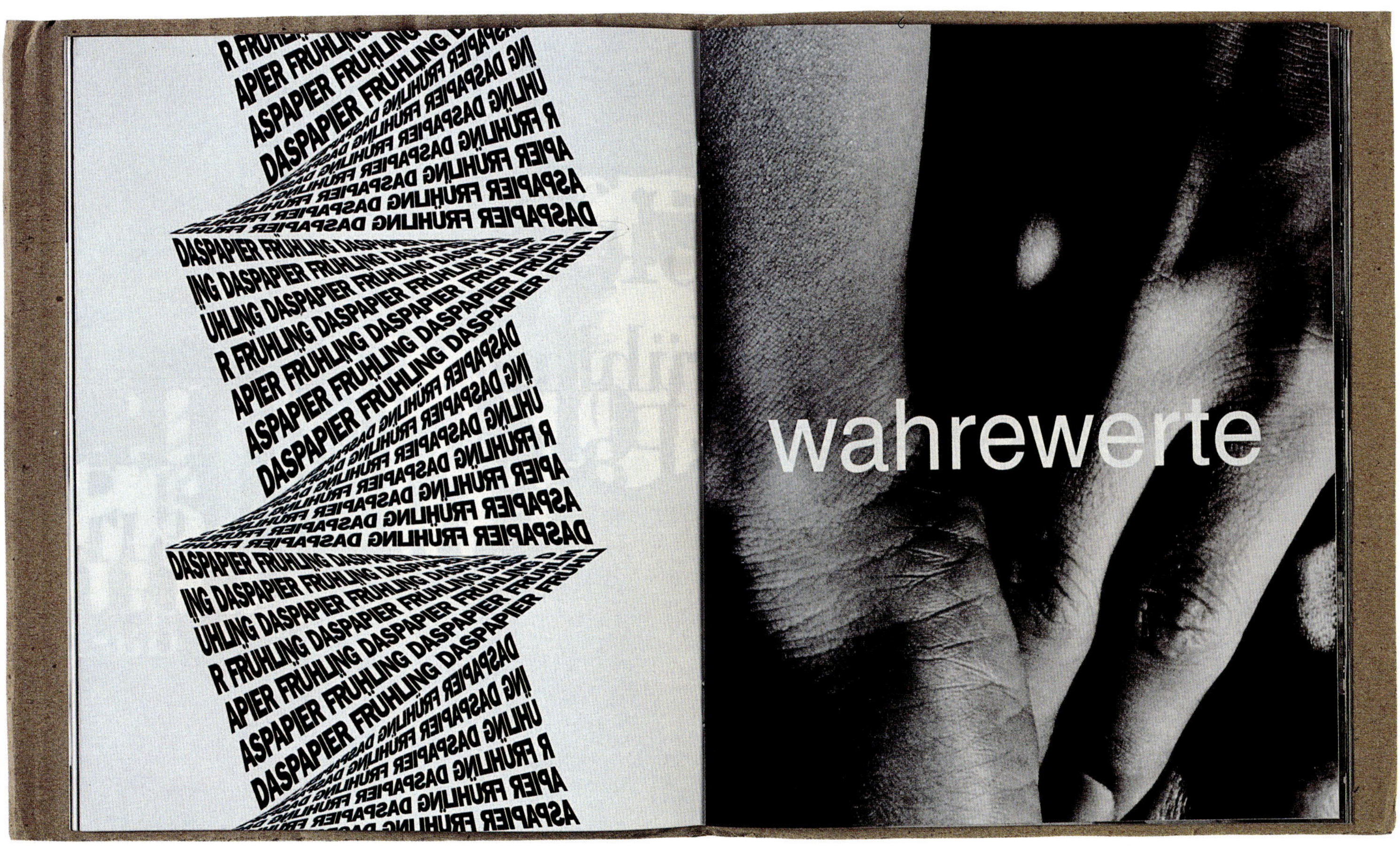

CD: Robert Bergman-Ungar D: Liong The CL: Das Papier Magazine USA 1993

CD, P: Robert Bergman-Ungar D: Liong The CL: Luaka Bop / Warner Bros. Records USA 1993

CD: Robert Bergman-Ungar P: Michel Comte / Bert Stern CL: Vogue Brasil USA 1992

sônia

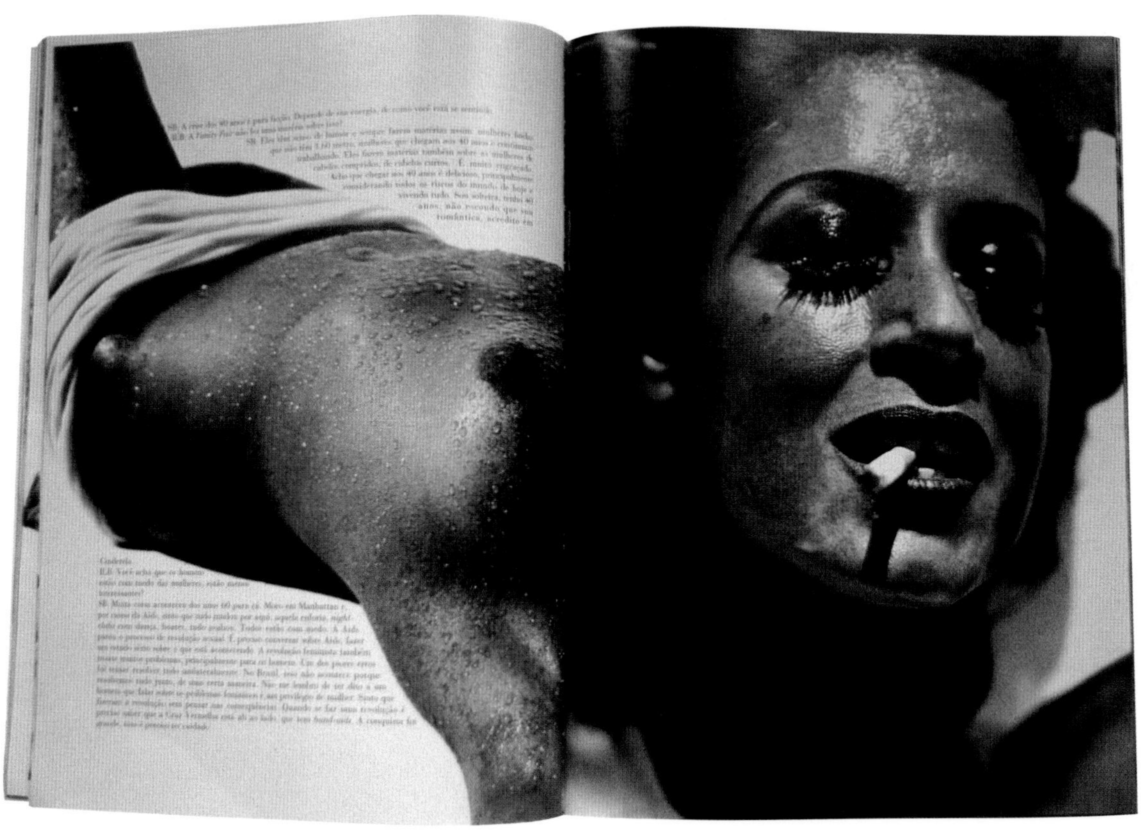

CD: Akira Notomo / Takumi Kato CD, AD: Yasuo Miki D: Hiroaki Nishida I: Manabu Yamanaka CL: Toshiba Japan 1990

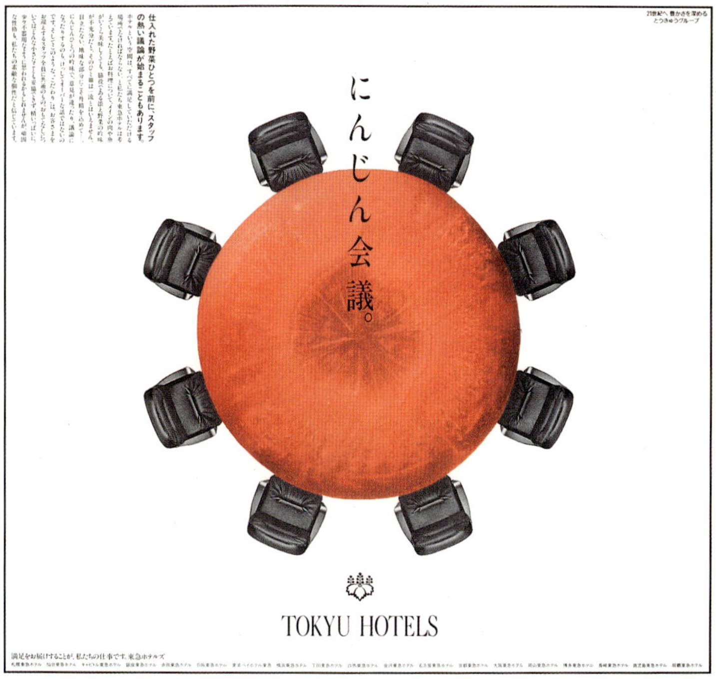

CD: Yuji Ogawa AD, D: Seichi Ohashi D: Toyoko Maeda P: Takuo Kusama DF: Les Mains CL: Tokyu Hotel Chain Japan 1991

CD: Ryoichi Fukuma AD, D: Seichi Ohashi D: Toyoko Maeda DF: Les Mains CL: Tokyu Hotel Chain Japan 1992

CD, AD, D: David Hurren / Ian Hutchings DF: Two CL: Eidos PLC England 1992

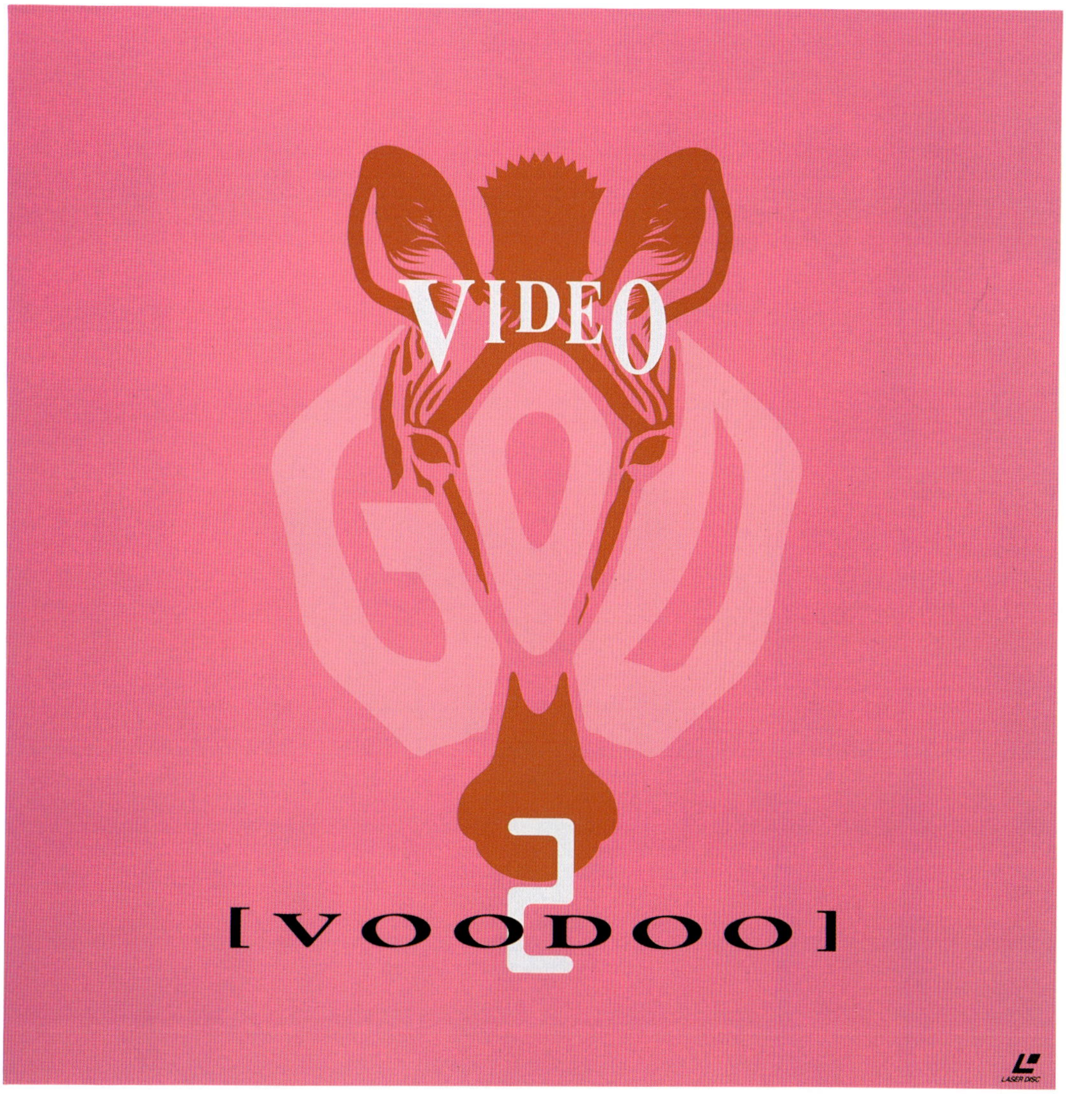

AD: Gento Matsumoto DF: Saru Brunei CL: Ask Kodansha Japan 1992

CD, AD, D, P: Ari Neufeld CD, AD, D: Breathless CL: Tenor Vossa Records England 1992

CD, AD, D: Michael Trudgeon DF: Crowd Productions CL: CSIRO Film and Video Cantre Australia 1991

S

CD: Robert Bergman-Ungar P: Michel Comte CL: Virgin Japan / Ryuichi Sakamoto USA 1990

CD, AD: André Toet D: Paul Chessel P: Paul Bogaers DF: Samenwerkende Ontwerpers CL: Drukkerij Mart. Spruijt The Netherlands 1993

AD: Kerry Burg D: Doug Keyes / Margo Sepanski / Susan Dewey / Stefanie Choi / Klindt Parker / Joe Cachero
CW: NBBJ DF: NBBJ (in-house graphic design group) CL: NBBJ USA 1992

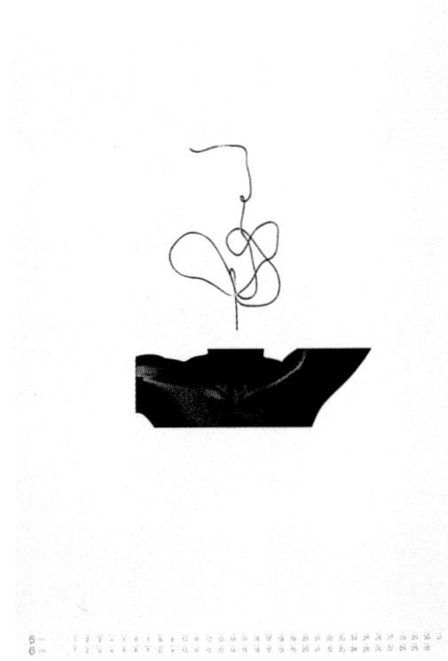

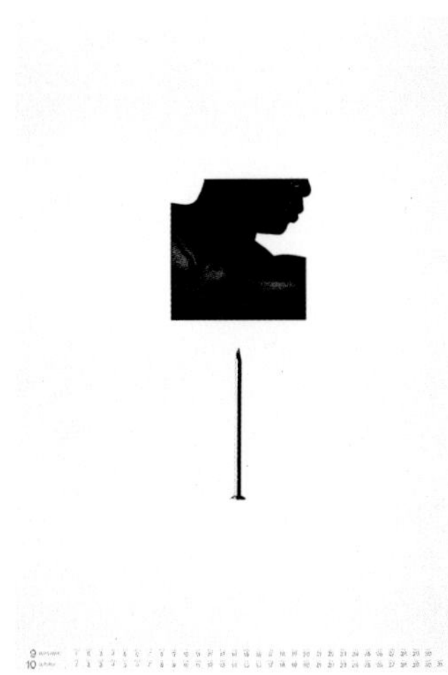

CD, AD, D: Kazunobu Kitakoga P: Masaru Kanai DF: Art Press Company CL: Art Press Company Japan 1992

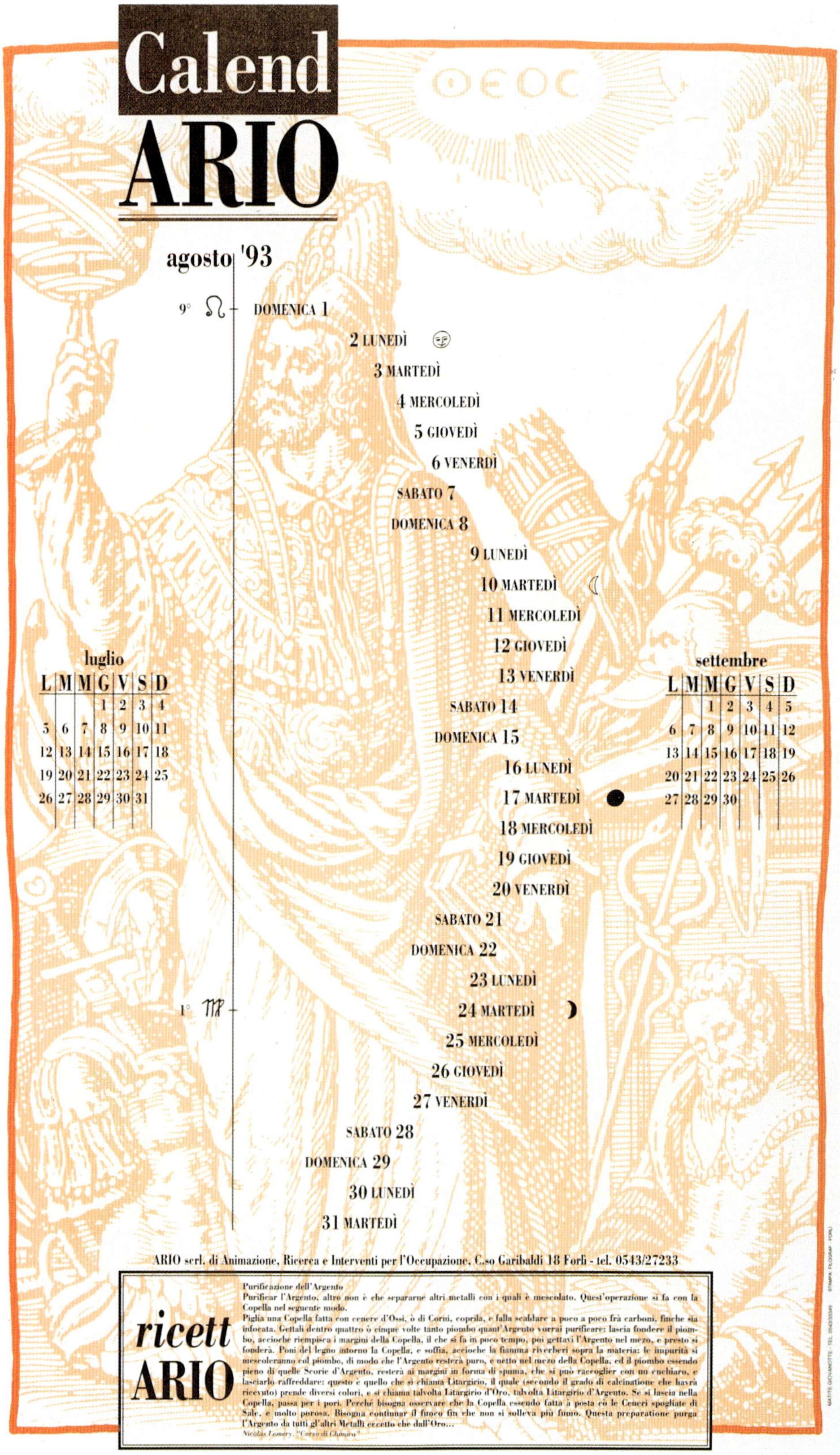

CD, AD: Barbara Longiardi DF: Matite Giovanotte CL: Coop. Ario Italy 1993

08

DGM

augustus 1991

31	32	33	34	35	
29	05	12	19	26	maandag
30	06	13	20	27	dinsdag
31	07	14	21	28	woensdag
01	08	15	22	29	donderdag
02	09	16	23	30	vrijdag
03	10	17	24	31	zaterdag
04	11	18	25	01	zondag

CD, D: Denise Ghering AD, CW: Arjon Oele P: Reinier Gerritsen DF: Ontwerpbureau Ghering CL: Ministrie VROM / DGM The Netherlands 1990

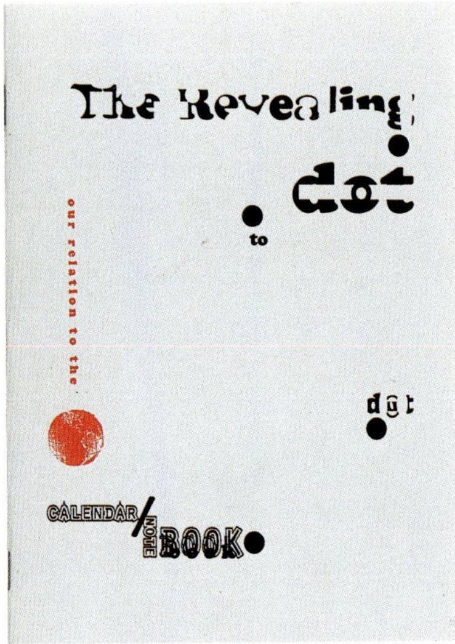

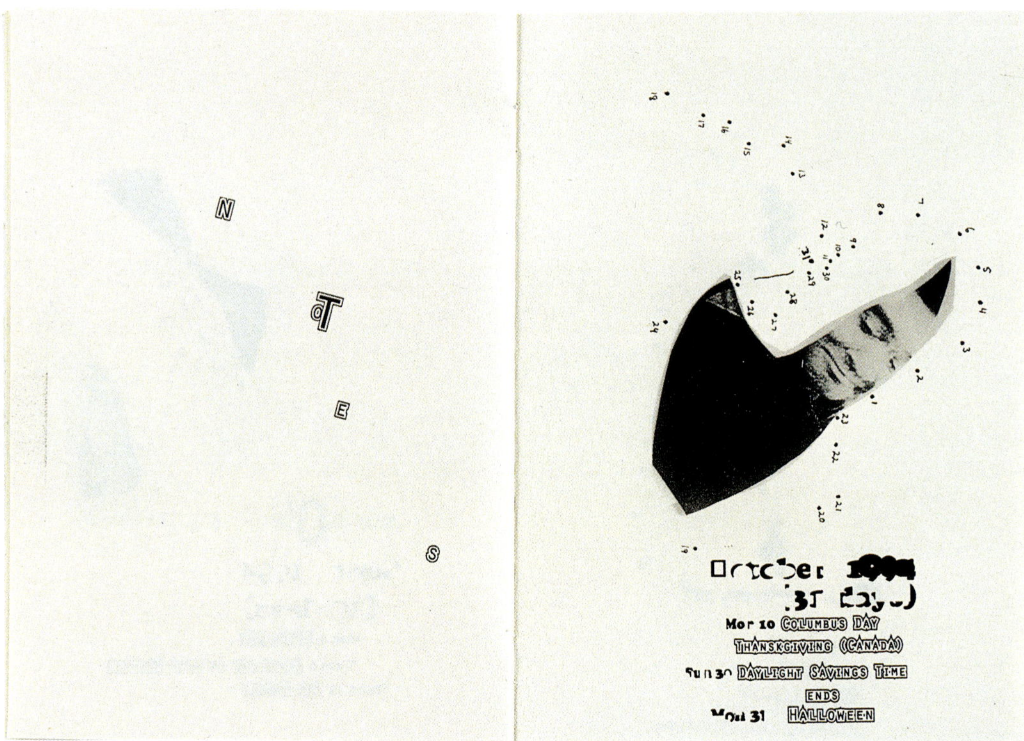

D: Fred Bower CL: Fred Bower USA 1993

A B C D

E F G H I J K L M N

SUBMITTOR'S INDEX

O

P

Q

R

S

T

U

V W X Y Z

A

AD·Able Group Mind Co., Ltd. 53
AIDMA Inc. 56
Alfalfa Design Studio Co., Ltd. 68, 77
ANCT, Imprimerie Nationale 18
Art Center College of Design 19
Art Chantry 22, 23, 25, 45, 49, 50
Art Press Company 197
ASA 100 Company 48, 145, 148, 171
Atelier Tadeusz Piechura 15

B

BBV 14, 59
BlackDog 44

C

Cabra Diseño 108, 109, 110
Charles S. Anderson Design Company 141
Clifford Stoltze Design 21, 179
Contemporary Production 185
Cranbrook Academy of Art 79, 86, 87, 91, 122, 167, 185, 200
Crowd Productions P/L 194

D

Darryl Kenwood Design 97
Design Club / Akihiko Tsukamoto 80, 94
design narrative 172
Design Quest Corporation 162
Dornig Grafik Design 103
Doug Gordon Design 169

E

elephant inc. 95
Emigre 29, 42, 113

F

Forsythe Design 74, 87, 173

G

Gardner + Greteman 24, 88
Guess?, Inc. 146, 147

H

Heter-O-Doxy Protprast 39
Hikita World Co., Ltd. 32
Hiromura Design Office, Inc. 38, 40, 41, 182
Hiroshi Seki 80

I

Isabelle Dervaux 67

J

J. Graham Hanson Graphic Design 123, 170

K

Kajitani Design Room 169
Kan Tai-keung Design & Associates Ltd. 163
Kato Shuzo Design Product Co., Ltd. 57
Katsunori Aoki / Sun-Ad Company Limited 16, 17, 28
Kazuya Kondo Inc. 160
Keisuke Unosawa 71, 75, 102, 126, 127
Kenzo Izutani Office Corporation 46
Kenzo Kobayashi 47
Kinema Moon designing 70
KINETIK Communication Graphics 134
Koeweiden / Postma 129
Koji Ise 160, 161
KROG 47

L

Les Mains Inc. / Seiichi Ohashi 191
Lutz Hans-Rudolf 44

M
M Plus M Incorporated 69, 72, 73, 92
Marc Lochs 84
Margo Sepanski 93
Matite Giovanotte 198
Melinda Beck 61, 66
Michael Stanard, Inc. 88
Mitani Ichiro Design Studio Inc. 36, 152, 153, 154, 155
Mitsunobu Murakami / Graphic Laboratory 182
Mizutani Studio 104, 144
Montse Hernãndez Sala bNO 75
Muller + Company 121, 136, 137, 138, 140

N
N. G. Inc. / Hiroaki Nagai 159
NBBJ 96, 114, 115, 124, 196
Naoki Sato / Tetsuzo 156, 158, 159, 163, 183, 184
Nice 130, 131, 132, 133
Nippon Design Center Inc. 190

O
Ontwerpbureau Ghering 199
Opera 150

P
Pentagram Design Ltd. 76
Peter Grundy Ownworks 12, 13
plus design inc. 102
Polystar Co., Ltd. 119
Proforma Rotterdam
85, 106, 107, 111, 112, 116, 117, 118, 119, 123, 125, 128, 175, 181

R
Ramona Hutko Design 55
Rickabaugh Graphics 101, 165
Ritchie Thorburn Design 151
Robert Bergman-Ungar Art Direction
27, 37, 143, 186, 187, 188, 189, 194

SUBMITTOR'S INDEX

S
Sabin Design 60
Samenwerkende Ontwerpers 195
Saru Brunei Co., Ltd. 33, 110, 193
Sayles Graphic Design 58, 120, 176, 177
SEGURA Inc.
64, 89, 90, 100, 122, 135, 170, 174, 178
Simon Sernec 15
Skolos / Wedell 10, 11, 34, 35
Sommese Design 65, 92, 98, 164
Spatchurst Design Associates 26
Stefanie Choi 93, 98
Steven Guarnaccia Studio 61, 62, 63, 83
Strehle GmbH & Co KG (Strenesse-Group) 149
Studio Bauman bNO 157
Studio Henrik Barends bNO 139, 168
Studio Seireeni 67, 78, 81, 142
Studio Super Compass Inc. 81, 99, 103, 105
Susumu Tada 183

T
Taylor & Browning Design Associates 124
Tenor Vossa Records 193
Trashline Studios 17, 43
Triom Design 54
Turquoise Design Inc. 51, 180
Two 82, 192

W
Willi Kunz Associates Inc. 20, 30, 31, 52

1, 2 & 3 COLOR GRAPHICS

Art Director
Kazuo Abe

Designers
Yutaka Ichimura
Shinji Ikenoue

Editors
Tsutomu Hirata
Ayako Aoyama
kaori Shibata
Kazuhisa Yoshihara
Yuko Yoshio

Editorial Manager
Masato Ieshiro

Coordinator
Chizuko Gilmore (San Francisco)

Photographer
Kuniharu Fujimoto

English Translator
write Away Co., Ltd.

Translators
Fuyuki Fujiwara
Pol Mahlow

Thanks to
Clive Avins
Douglas Allsopp
Naomi Sakuma
Rie Okada
Publisher
Shingo Miyoshi

1993年 9月25日初版第 1刷発行

定価 16,000 円（本体15,534円）

発行所 ピエ・ブックス
〒170 東京都豊島区駒込4-14-6-407
TEL: 03-3949-5010 FAX: 03-3949-5650

製版・印刷・製本（株）飛来社
〒162 東京都新宿区若松町38-23 和幸マンション
TEL: 03-5272-3651 FAX: 03-5272-3617

ISBN 4-938586-46-0 C3070 P16000E

P·I·E Books, as always, has several new and ambitious graphic book projects in the works which will introduce a variety of superior designs from Japan and abroad. Currently we are planning the collection series detailed below. If you have any graphics which you consider worthy for submission to these publications, please fill in the necessary information on the inserted questionnaire postcard and forward it to us. You will receive a notice when the relevant project goes into production.

REQUEST FOR SUBMISSIONS

A. Postcard Graphics
B. Advertising Greeting Cards
C. Brochure & Pamphlet Collection
D. Poster Graphics
E. Book Cover and Editorial Design
F. Corporate Image Design
G. Business Card and Letterhead Graphics
H. Calendar Graphics
I. Packaging and Wrapping Graphics

ピエ・ブックスでは、今後も新しいタイプのグラフィック書籍の出版を目指すとともに、国内外の優れたデザインを幅広く紹介していきたいと考えております。今後の刊行予定として下記のコレクション・シリーズを企画しておりますので、作品提供していただける企画がございましたら、挟み込みのアンケートハガキに必要事項をご記入の上お送り下さい。企画が近づきましたらそのつど案内書をお送りいたします。

作品提供のお願い

A.ポストカード・グラフィックス
B.アドバタイジング・グリーティングカード
C.ブローシュア & パンフレット・コレクション
D.ポスター・グラフィックス
E.ブックカバー&エディトリアル・デザイン
F.コーポレイト・イメージ & ロゴマーク・デザイン
G.ビジネスカード&レターヘッド・グラフィックス
H.カレンダー・グラフィックス
I. パッケージ&ラッピング・グラフィックス

Comme toujours, P·I·E Books a dans ses ateliers plusieurs projets de livres graphiques neufs et ambitieux qui introduiront une gamme de modèles supérieurs en provenance du Japon et de l'étranger. Nous prévoyons en ce moment la série de collections détaillée cidessous. Si vous êtes en possession d'un graphique que vous jugez digne de soumettre à ces publications, nous vous prions de remplir les informations nécessaires sur l'étiquette à renvoyer située à la carte postale questionnaire insérée et de nous la faire parvenir. Vous recevrez un avis lorsque le projet correspondant passera à la production.

DEMANDE DE SOUMISSIONS

A. Graphiques pour cartes postales
B. Cartes de voeux publicitaires
C. Collection de brochures et de pamphlets
D. Graphiques sur affiche
E. Designs de couverture de livre et d'éditorial
F. Designs de logo d'image de société
G. Graphiques pour en-têtes et cartes de visite
H. Graphiques pour calendrier
I. Graphiques pour emballage et paquetage

Wie immer hat P·I·E Books einige neue anspruchsvolle Grafikbücher in Arbeit, die eine Vielzahl von hervorragenden Designs aus Japan und anderen Ländern vorstellen werden. Momentan planen wir eine Serie mit den nachfolgend aufgeführten Themen. Wenn Sie grafische Darstellungen besitzen, von denen Sie meinen, daß sie in diese Veröffentlichung aufgenommen werden könten, geben Sie uns bitte die nötigen Informationen auf der entsprechenden Antwortseite am füllen Sie die beigelegte Antwortkarte aus und schicken Sie sie an uns. Wir werden Sie benachrichtigen, wenn das entsprechende Projekt in Arbeit geht.

AUFFORDERUNG ZU MITARBEIT

A. Postkarten-Grafik
B. Werbe-Grußkarten
C. Zusammenstellung von Broschüren und Druckschriften
D. Postergrafik
E. Bucheinbände und redaktionelles Design
F. Corporate-Image-Logo-Design
G.Visitenkarten und Briefkopf-Grafik
H. Kalendergrafik
I. Grafik auf Verpackungen und Verpackungsmaterial

THE P·I·E COLLECTION

ADVERTISING GREETING CARDS 1
Pages: 224(144 in color) ¥15,000
業種別ダイレクトメールの集大成
A collection of more than 500 direct mail pieces selected from thousands used throughout Japan. Cards were selected for their distinctive design and include 3-D pop-ups, special die-cuts, folds and embossings.

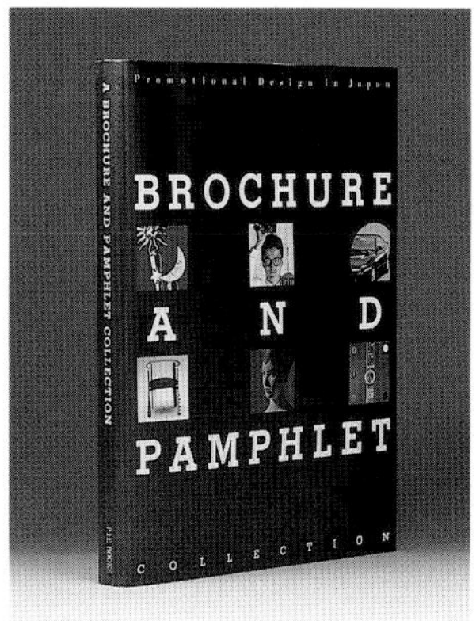

BROCHURE & PAMPHLET COLLECTION 1
Pages: 224(144 in color) ¥15,000
業種別カタログ・コレクション
Here are hundreds of the best brochures and pamphlets from Japan.
This collection will make a valuable sourcebook for anyone involved in corporate identity advertising and graphic design.

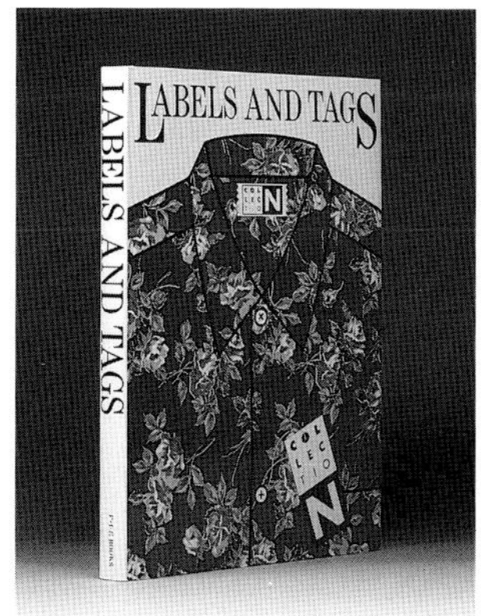

LABELS AND TAGS
Pages: 224(192 in color) ¥15,000
ファッションのラベル&タグ・コレクション
Over 1,600 garment labels representing 450 brands produced in Japan are included in this full-color collection.

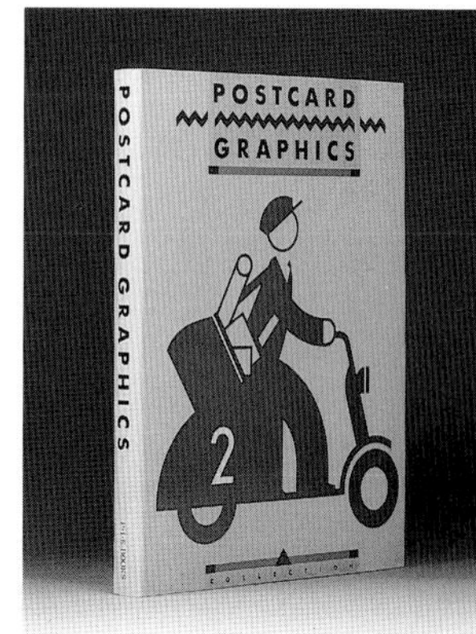

POSTCARD GRAPHICS 2
Pages: 240(208 in color) ¥16,000
好評！ 業種別ポストカードの第２弾
Here are 1,500 promotional postcards created by Japan's top design talent.
A wide range of clients are represented including 120 fashion houses and 90 major retailers. Presented in striking full color.

BUSINESS CARD GRAPHICS 1
Pages: 256(160 in color) ¥16,000
世界の名刺&ショップカード集大成
Over 1,200 business cards are presented in this international collection.
Created by 500 of the world's top design firms, designers will discover a wealth of new ideas in this remarkable collection.

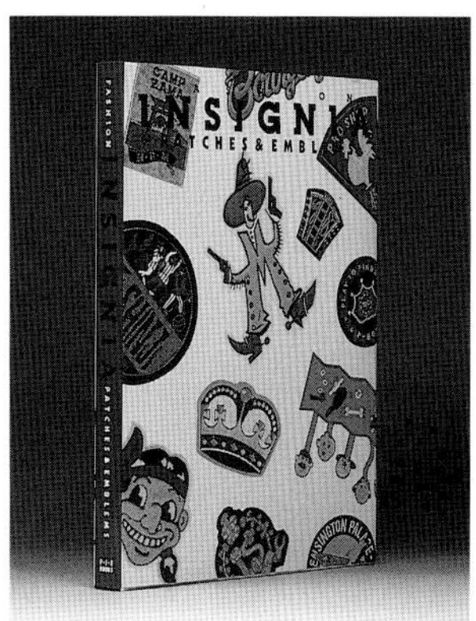

FASHION INSIGNIA
Pages: 224(208 in color) ¥16,000
ファッションのワッペン・コレクション
One thousand full-color emblems have been gathered in this beautiful and sometimes playful collection.
The great variety of color and shape demonstrates the versatility of embroidery art.

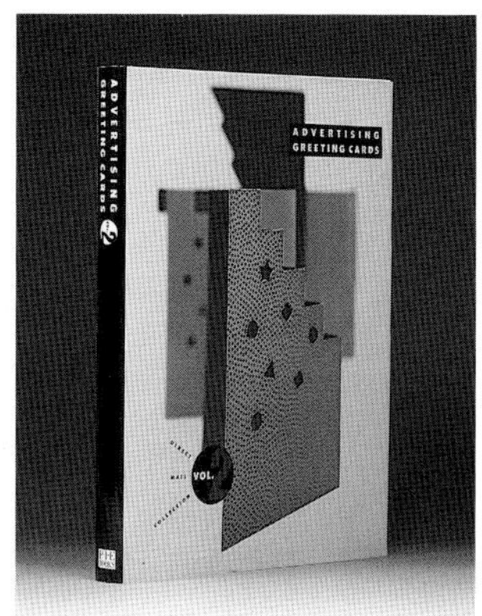

ADVERTISING GREETING CARDS 2
Pages: 224(176 in color) ¥16,000
世界のダイレクトメール・コレクション
500 visually remarkable works representing a variety of businesses.
Pieces include new product announcements, invitation cards and direct mail envelopes. An excellent image bank for graphic designers.

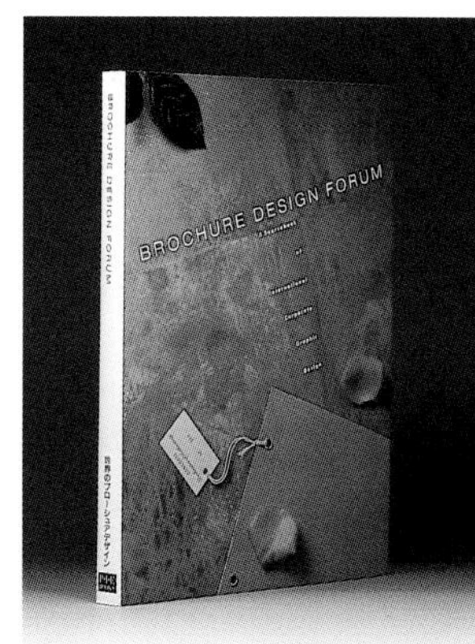

BROCHURE DESIGN FORUM 1
Pages: 224(192 in color) ¥15,000
世界のカタログ・コレクション
A large collection of international brochures from a variety of business categories. Showcases more than 250 eye-catching works.

COVER TO COVER
Pages: 240(176 in color) ¥17,000
世界のブック&エディトリアル・デザイン
The latest trends in book and magazine design are illustrated with over 1,000 creative works by international firms.

BUSINESS STATIONERY GRAPHICS 1
Pages: 224(192 in color) ¥15,000
世界のレターヘッド・コレクション
Creatively designed letterheads, business cards, memo pads, and other business forms and documents are included this international collection.

MUSIGRAPHICS 1
Pages: 224(192 in color) ¥16,000
世界のＬＰ&ＣＤグラフィックス
A collection of more than 600 of the world's most outstanding CD and LP covers, featuring design for all musical genres.

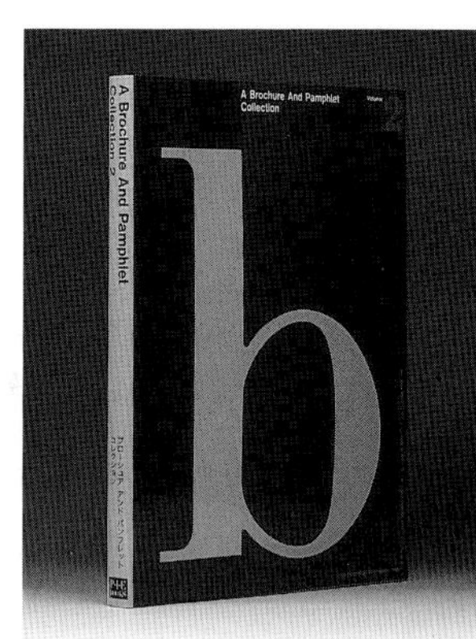

BROCHURE & PAMPHLET COLLECTION 2
Pages: 224(192 in color) ¥15,000
業種別カタログ・コレクション、第２弾
Features a selection of 1,000 brochures and pamphlets covering a wide range of products from Japan. The value of brochures in visual communication is demonstrated in this dazzling collection.

THE P·I·E COLLECTION

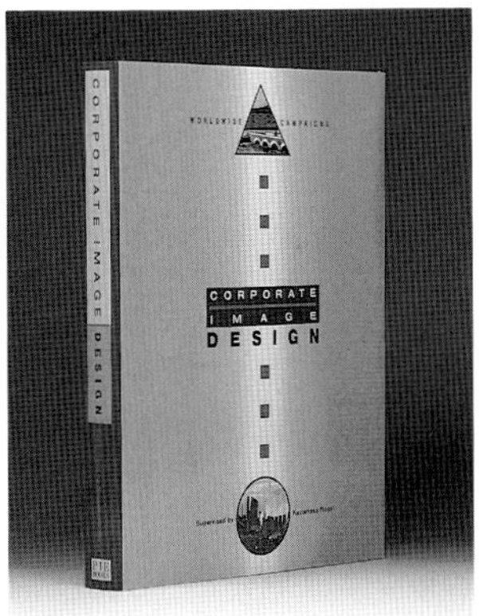

CORPORATE IMAGE DESIGN
Pages: 336(272 in color) ¥16,000
世界の業種別ＣＩ・ロゴマーク
This collection presents the best corporate identity projects from around the world. Creative and effective designs from top international firms are featured in this valuable source book.

POSTCARD GRAPHICS 3
Pages: 232(208 in color) ¥16,000
世界の業種別ポストカード・コレクション
Volume 3 in the series presents more than 1,200 promotional postcards in dazzling full color. Top designers from the world over have contributed to this useful image bank of ideas.

GRAPHIC BEAT London / Tokyo 1 & 2
Pages: 224(208 in color) ¥16,000
音楽とグラフィックのコラボレーション
1,500 music-related graphic works from 29 of the hottest designers in Tokyo and London. Features Malcolm Garrett,Russell Miles, Tadanori Yokoo, Neville Brody, Vaughn Oliver and others.

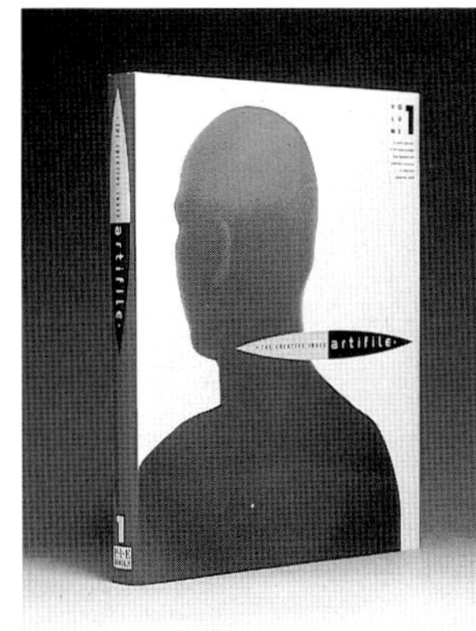

The Creative Index ARTIFILE 1
Pages: 224(Full color) ¥12,500
実力派プロダクション104社の作品集
Showcases the best works from 104 graphic studios in Japan and abroad. A variety of fields included such as advertising design, corporate identity, photography and illustration.

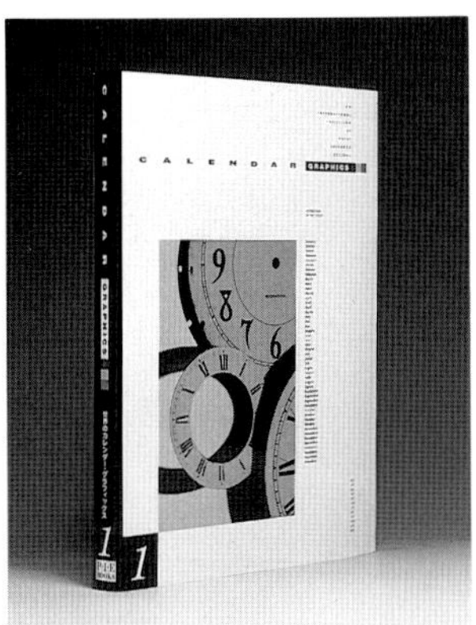

CALENDAR GRAPHICS
Pages: 224(192 in color) ¥16,000
世界のカレンダー・グラフィックス
An exciting collection of creatively designed calendars from around the world. A wide variety of styles included such as poster, book and 3-D calendars. Clients range from large corporations to retail shops.

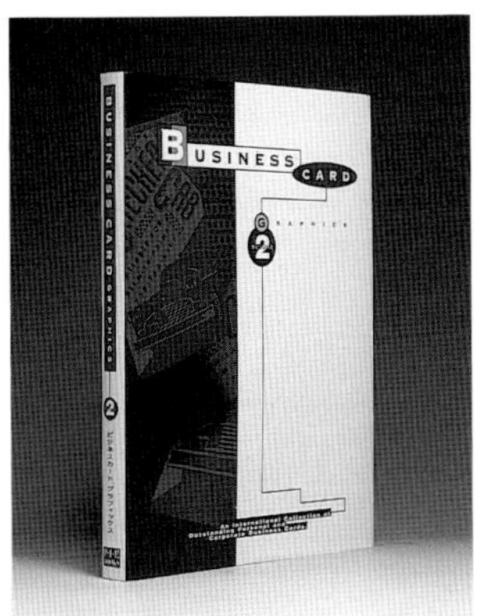

BUSINESS CARD GRAPHICS 2
Pages: 224(192 in color) ¥16,000
世界の名刺&ショップカード、第２弾
This latest collection presents 1,000 creative cards from international designers. Features hundreds of cards used in creative fields such as graphic design and architecture.

T-SHIRT GRAPHICS
Pages: 224(192 in color) ¥16,000
世界のＴシャツ・グラフィックス
This unique collection showcases 700 wonderfully creative T-Shirt designs from the world's premier design centers. Grouped according to theme, categories include sports, casual, designer and promotional shirts among others.

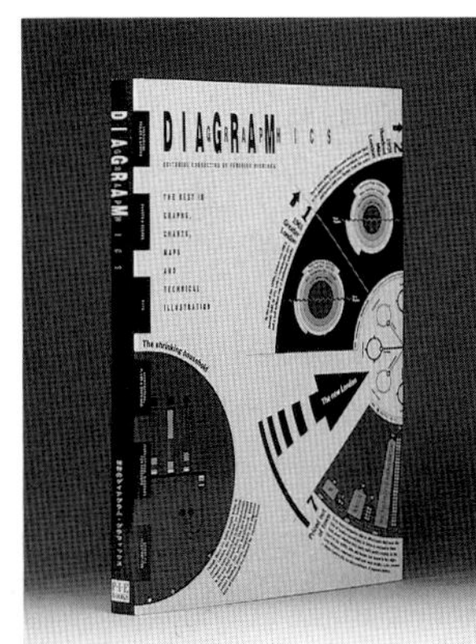

DIAGRAM GRAPHICS
Pages: 224(192 in color) ¥16,000
世界のダイアグラム・デザインの集大成
Hundreds of unique ahd lucid diagrams, charts, graphs, maps and technical illustrations from leading international design firms. Variety of media represented including computer graphics.

SPECIAL EVENT GRAPHICS
Pages: 224(192 in color) ¥16,000
世界のイベント・グラフィックス特集
This innovative collection features design elements from concerts, festivals, fashion shows, symposiums and more. International works include posters, tickets, flyers, invitations and various premiers.

PACKAGING DESIGN & GRAPHICS 1
Pages: 224(192 in color) ¥16,000
世界の業種別パッケージ・デザイン
An international collection featuring 400 creative and exciting package designs from renowned designers.

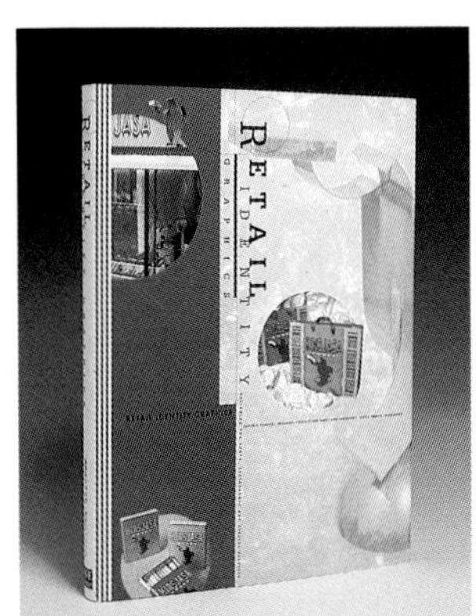

RETAIL IDENTITY GRAPHICS
Pages: 208(176 in color) ¥14,800
世界のショップ・グラフィックス
This visually exciting collection showcases the identity design campaigns of restaurants, bars, shops and various other retailers. Wide variety of pieces are featured including business cards, signs, menus, bags and hundreds more.

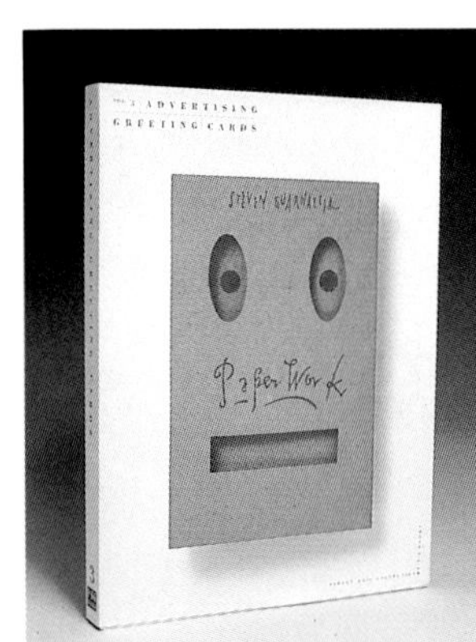

ADVERTISING GREETING CARDS 3
Pages: 224(176 in color) ¥16,000
世界のダイレクトメール集大成、第3弾
The best-selling series continues with this collection of elegantly designed advertising pieces from a wide variety of categories. This exciting image bank of ideas will interest all graphic designers and direct mail specialists.

THE P·I·E COLLECTION

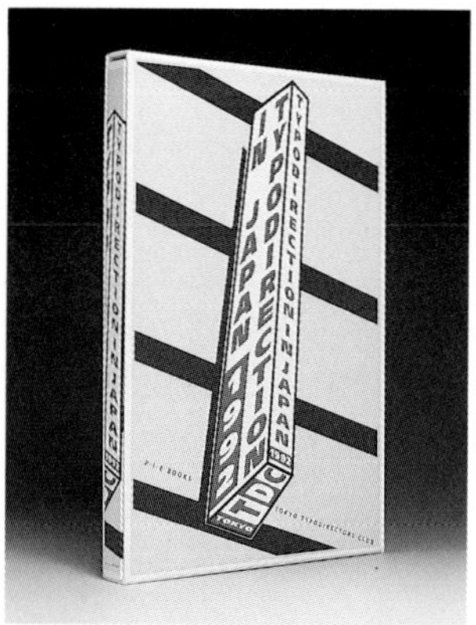

TYPODIRECTION IN JAPAN 4
Pages: 254(183 in color) ¥17,000
年鑑 日本のタイポディレクション **'92**
314 award-winning works of outstanding typographical art from Japan and abroad. Included, you will find up-to-the-minute examples of concept-development works and previously unpublished typefaces from top art dirctors and graphic designers.

NEW TYPO GRAPHICS
Pages: 224(192 in color) ¥16,000
世界の最新タイポグラフィ・コレクション
New and innovative typographical works gathered from top designers around the world. A wide variety of type applications are shown including posters, Brochures, CD jackets, calendars, package designs and more.

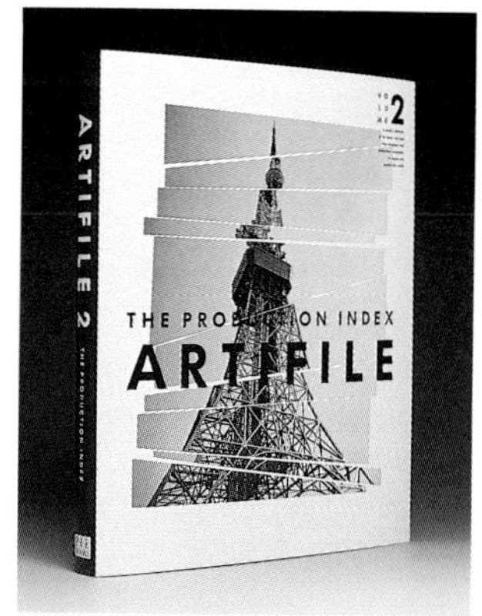

The Production Index ARTIFILE 2
Pages: 244(240 in color) ¥13,500
活躍中！ 最新プロダクション年鑑、第２弾
A design showcase featuring the best works from 115 graphic design studios, photographers, and creators in Japan. Works shown include print advertisements, corporate identity pieces, commercial photography and illustration.